············ the joy of keeping ············

horses

The Ultimate Guide to Keeping Horses on Your Property

··

Jessie Shiers

Skyhorse Publishing

Skyhorse Publishing books may be purchased in bulk at
special discounts for sales promotion, corporate gifts,
fund-raising, or educational purposes. Special editions
can also be created to specifications. For details, contact
the Special Sales Department, Skyhorse Publishing,
307 West 36th Street, 11th Floor, New York, NY 10018 or
info@skyhorsepublishing.com.

Skyhorse® and Skyhorse Publishing® are registered
trademarks of Skyhorse Publishing, Inc.®, a Delaware
corporation.

Visit our website at www.skyhorsepublishing.com.

10 9 8 7 6 5 4 3 2 1

Library of Congress Cataloging-in-Publication Data is
available on file.
ISBN: 978-1-61608-424-0

Printed in China

CONTENTS

PART ③

HORSE CARE

Introduction

An owner once said that his horse reminded him of a
lightning rod, for, as he rode, all the sorrows of his heart
flowed down through the splendid muscles of his horse and
were grounded in the earth.

—Marguerite Henry, *Album of Horses*

ONE MIGHT THINK that after more than two decades of
horse-craziness, including researching and writing several horse
books, I might know all there is to know about horses—or at least *think*
I know all there is to know! In reality, this couldn't be further from the
truth. I learn new things about horses literally every day that I spend
with them. Each horse and each situation offers a new opportunity to
learn. The important thing is not knowing it all, but rather admitting
that you don't, and being willing and in fact excited to research and
learn constantly. Read magazines, peruse websites, and talk to your
vet, farrier, and horse friends about the latest developments in horse
health, nutrition, training, and management.

Horses Can Save You Money!

Things you will have to "sacrifice" when you have horses:

Gym membership: Trust me, you won't have time for it. And you really won't need to be working out at the gym—you'll be getting all the exercise you need by mucking stalls, pushing wheelbarrows, stacking hay bales, lugging water . . . oh, and of course, riding!

Expensive car: Ditch the high monthly payment for a luxury sedan and trade it in for a beater with a hatchback. You will just be mucking it up with shavings and grain bags, muddy boots, filthy horse blankets, and dirty saddle pads. Plus, you'll need to save up for a new truck. And trailer.

Nice clothes: Umm . . . no. You might as well start shopping at Goodwill now. You will not be able to make it from your front door to the car without having to stop by the paddock, where you will become covered in hay chaff, manure, and horse slobber (how can you resist those nose kisses?). There's no point in trying to dress nicely. You will fail.

Dinners out: Fine dining is simply a luxury, and one for which you will have neither time nor money when you have horses at home. Far better to make good use of your Crock-Pot to prepare quick, healthy, inexpensive meals at home.

Vacations: You'll be spending your summers riding and showing. Plus, unless you have a really excellent horse sitter available, you won't want to leave your farm for more than a couple of days at a time.

Why Keep Horses?

This is a very valid question. After all, horses are quite expensive to own and extremely time-consuming to care for. Why would anyone dump so much money and time down the drain? Non-horse people often simply don't get it. When considering the answer to this question, I realized there are actually two components to it: Why have horses at all? and Why keep them at home, when it can be so much easier to board them at a stable? I will address each part separately.

Why Own and Ride Horses at All?

For many of us horse-crazy individuals, horses simply seem to be hard-wired into our brains and hearts. Many have loved horses since we were old enough to say the word "horsie." They are the stuff of childhood fantasy made real. We can't ride dragons or befriend unicorns, but horses—horses are real! Strong, beautiful, sensitive, fast, muscular, with arching necks and flagging tails . . . they seem

ABOVE Kids who have horses learn about compassion and responsibility at an early age.

ABOVE: The sight of a beautiful horse galloping at liberty can lift the spirits.

almost mythical. Yet we can touch them, interact with them, even ride them.

As young pony lovers grow older, they have many life lessons to learn from horses. Owning a horse requires a great deal of responsibility. A horse can teach a teenager the value of hard work, as well as the value of compassion and caring for another living being. She learns how to be sensitive to the needs and feelings of another and how to focus on the task at hand. If she competes at horse shows, a rider learns how to win gracefully, how to accept defeat, how to learn from her mistakes and move on, and how to take responsibility for her own actions and never to blame her horse.

On the practical side, a young rider who is entering high school is facing a world of temptations, not all of them positive. If riding brings her happiness and satisfaction, she will choose going to the barn after school to spend time with her animals and her barn friends, rather than potentially getting into mischief. If she knows she has to be up at 6 AM on Saturday to get ready for a horse show, she's not likely to stay out late on Friday night partying. These types of associations and habits will stay with her throughout her life, leading her into positive social involvements rather than negative ones.

For many adults, horses serve as a form of emotional therapy. A common saying is, "Hay is less expensive than a psychiatrist." What does this mean, exactly? Well, it can mean different things to different people.

At the simplest level, a horse is a source of sheer physical beauty. Many people find spiritual solace from admiring artwork, gazing at the sunset over the ocean, or watching a dance performance. Horses can bring us the same sense of peace and wonder. As we watch them grazing calmly in the pasture, their sense of peace and contentment radiates into us. As we witness a herd galloping across a field in unison, their power and grace overwhelm us. Watching a horse and rider act as one mind and one body to dance through a series of movements in a dressage test or reining pattern has literally brought tears to my eyes. (If you want to experience this for yourself, search YouTube for videos of Andreas Helgstrand and Blue Hors Matiné's Grand Prix Freestyle dressage test at the 2006 World Equestrian Games, or Stacy Westfall's winning freestyle reining ride at the 2006 Quarter Horse Congress.)

Delving a little deeper, horses are extremely sensitive, emotional creatures that can channel our own emotional states. As prey animals that live in herds, they have evolved to be tuned in to the emotional states of their companions or risk being left behind when the herd flees from danger. A horse knows when you are tense, stressed, anxious, or frightened. He also knows when you're sad, depressed, or angry. A good horse knows when you need a hug or a strong, soft shoulder to cry on. He knows when you're happy and ready to play. He knows when you're focused and ready to work. Humans are social

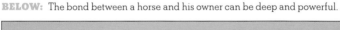

BELOW: The bond between a horse and his owner can be deep and powerful.

animals, too, and we crave this kind of emotional feedback. A horse can be a dear friend, a trusted ally, providing that emotional connection that makes us feel secure.

This is all getting a bit heady. Lest we forget, the best thing about horses is that they're so much fun! It's darn near impossible to feel depressed when you're galloping on the beach, the wind in your face and a mane in your hands. Riding a horse is an activity that quickly puts you in the zone—you're riding, and nothing else. Whether it's a relaxing trail ride, an exhilarating gallop around a course of fences, or an intense, focused riding lesson, once in the saddle you stop worrying about the bills, the pressures of work, social dramas, the challenges of parenting, the mean teacher from school, or anything else that may be weighing on you. Horse time is a break from all of that stress.

Why Keep Them at Home Rather Than at a Stable?

So we've established that horses have their benefits. But isn't it easier to keep them at a stable, rather than at home? Why put all that energy and labor into caring for them ourselves when we could just pay someone to do it at the barn? Well, for many people, that is the choice they make. For those of us reading this book, there may be added benefits to bringing our horses home to live with us.

For my husband and me, keeping horses is part of a larger lifestyle that we have consciously chosen for our family. We cut, split, and burn our own firewood from our woodlot, thereby clearing land that will later become more pasture for our horses or perhaps a site for a future barn or arena. We grow our own vegetables in our large garden, which is fertilized by composted horse manure. We keep several egg-laying hens, who keep our horses company while picking through the paddocks to eliminate ticks and other insects. They also scratch up the manure piles in the pastures, which allows the manure to dry in the sun, killing fly and parasite eggs while adding nutrients to the soil.

The horses bring us out of the house and into nature every day, rain or shine, blizzard or blistering heat. Recently I went outside at 10:30 on a perfect, sharply cold, brilliantly starry winter evening to fill the water trough, which my horse Beamer had once again tipped over. Standing there waiting for the hose to fill the trough, in the paddock amid the smells of the horses and the glow of starlight off the ice-crusted snow, I realized that I would never have experienced this moment of stillness if I did not have animals that needed tending. It is these moments of joy that epitomize the reasons we keep horses, reasons that can't fully be expressed in words.

Another benefit of having horses at home is that we can often give them better, more individualized care than they would receive at a large boarding stable. This is not to say that the care at boarding stables can't be good—it can often be excellent. But one or two barn workers caring for ten or twenty horses can't possibly give each one the individual attention he could receive from his owner at home.

BELOW: Horses bring us joy!

RIGHT: Lessons with a well-qualified instructor are the best way to learn about horses and horse care.

We also get to know our horses and their unique quirks and moods better than we could if they lived elsewhere, being cared for by workers. For example, I know my horses well enough to be able to sense with some accuracy when a problem is going to occur. I can tell from their facial expressions when something is bothering them physically, even before the onset of any observable symptoms. One evening, for example, after feeding dinner and tucking the horses in for the night, I noticed Beamer looked . . . funny. He wasn't doing anything unusual, and he'd eaten his grain without any problems, but I could tell from the look on his face that something wasn't right. Later that evening I decided to go out and check on him, since I sensed that he wasn't feeling well. I found him colicking in his stall. Another time, I felt there was something off about my mare Robin. She wasn't lame, and, like Beamer, had no visible symptoms. But she had that same introspective look on her face that told me something in her body wasn't right. The next day, she was dead lame from an abscess in her right hind.

How to Get Into Horses

This book is written for people who already own or lease horses and keep them in a boarding situation, or at least have taken lessons for several years and are educated on the basics. If you don't know much about horses and picked up this book because you think a horse might be a fun addition to your small farm; if you've dreamed of owning a horse all your life but have never had the chance to learn to ride; or if your young children are begging for a pony, and the backyard does seem big enough to keep one in; then by all means, read on for inspiration and education. But before you take the plunge into actual horse ownership, I strongly advise that you find a reputable riding stable and start taking lessons.

Let your instructor know that ownership is your eventual goal, and ask her to tailor your lessons so that you learn as much as possible, not only about riding, but about horse care and horsemanship. You can also ask your instructor or the barn's manager to give you an "internship," a supervised hands-on course in stable management. Learn to tack and untack, clean tack, muck stalls, groom and pick hooves, take a horse's pulse and respiration, clean a sheath, and so forth. Be there when the vet and farrier come, and ask questions. In short, learn first-hand what caring for a horse is all about.

If it is your children who are horse-crazy, be sure to attend their lessons and absorb all the information they are learning; don't just drop them off and go run errands while they ride. Even better, ask if you or your children can work off part of their lesson costs by doing chores at the barn. They'll learn the basics of horse care on the job.

Once you have several months of lessons under your belt, it may be time to consider leasing or buying a horse or pony. The best way to ease into horse ownership is to find a good lease situation. Perhaps there is a boarder at your barn who can't find time to ride her horse as much as she'd like, or a young rider who is going off to college but doesn't want to sell her old show pony. Ask your trainer to help you find the right match. Leasing allows you to get a sense of the expenses and responsibilities of horse ownership, but retains the "bail factor." If your work situation suddenly changes and you can't afford the horse anymore, you can bail. If the horse comes up lame and can no longer be ridden, you can bail. If you discover, over time, that this whole horse-owning business just isn't working out for you, you can bail. If the kids lose interest and want to start playing soccer instead, you can bail. It's not your horse.

After leasing for a while, you will eventually find that you really yearn for a horse of your own. You've been riding for several years now, and you've learned a lot about daily care and horsemanship from your trainer. You now feel that you are ready to take that next step and start looking for a horse to buy. Great! Turn to Part 1 and start figuring out what steps you need to take to get your property ready to bring home your new best friend. Once that's done, it's time to enlist your trainer's help and start horse shopping!

My Story

Throughout the book, I've interspersed profiles of horsekeepers I know. I wanted to offer a variety of different perspectives and different ways of doing things. As a reader, you may be curious about me and my horse experience, so here I'll share my story.

From a young age I was always fascinated with horses. After begging my parents, I started taking riding lessons at age nine. From my first instructor, who rode and taught Western, I learned what a bit was, how to brush a horse, and how to mount, among other things. Before long that first instructor went off to college and I moved on to another stable in the area, one that happened to have a focus on eventing. There I stayed for the next ten years, under the tutelage of Mott Atherholt and her daughter, Caroline Atherholt, who went on to become an Advanced eventer competing at the international level. Mott and Caroline valued the importance of the horse care side of learning to ride, and made sure all of their students knew and respected the time-honored methods of stable management. During each summer's pony camp week, after morning chores we were subjected to barn inspections by Caroline. Woe be unto the camper whose stall wasn't immaculate or whose grain bucket remained unscrubbed! We also had a weekly horse inspection, for which we had to clean our tack until it gleamed and groom our horses to the nines. Caroline and Mott devised such educational methods as having the campers race to take apart, clean, and reassemble a bridle—blindfolded. Does this all sound dreadful? On the contrary—I was having the time of my life.

In later years I served as a working student for Mott, cleaning stalls and scrubbing buckets in exchange for lesson time. I also leased a horse for two years, a 14.2-hand bay Arabian/Quarter Horse mare named Bridget, whom I kept at my home.

After major surgery during my senior year of high school, there was a bit of a lull in my equestrian activities. In college I rode on the equestrian team, which gave me experience riding a variety of different horses. By the end of my college career, I'd found myself a job as a stall mucker, farm sitter, and occasional up-down instructor at a local hunter/jumper stable. I worked and rode there for several years, cleaning fourteen stalls a day and riding as much as I could. In 2003 I married my husband, Jason, and soon after that, with my trainer's help, I bought my first horse, George, a four-year-old off-the-track Thoroughbred, who kept growing until he was 16.3 hands.

I got my first job in publishing as an intern at Globe Pequot Press in 2002. Over the next few years, I developed my career in the publishing industry at Globe Pequot and then its sister company Lyons Press, moving up the ranks while being fortunate enough to assist with the Lyons Press equestrian list, working with such notables as William Steinkraus and Buck Brannaman. I was surrounded by books about horses, riding, and horsekeeping, and every night I went to the barn on the way home and rode my own horse.

Eventually circumstances warranted a move to a new barn, where I continued to work with George and also met my next equine partner, Beamer, a 16.1-hand five-year-old chestnut Appendix gelding. After a

BELOW: George and me in 2004.

BELOW: Beamer and me on a winter trail ride in 2010.

series of unfortunate life changes left him mentally shaken and virtually unrideable (as he bucked everyone off), I was able to buy him at a fraction of his earlier value. I knew his history and knew that under the surface, his earlier good training was still there. He just needed a little time, patience, and consistency. My intention was to "fix him" and then sell him. Unfortunately (or perhaps fortunately) by the time he was fixed, I had fallen in love, and never did sell him.

In 2006 my husband and I decided the time had come for us to look for a farm of our own. With two horses, we were paying more than $1,000 a month in board, so we figured if we had our own place, we could put that money toward a mortgage. Property in Connecticut is shockingly expensive, and was even more so at the time, at the peak of the housing bubble, so we quickly discovered that we couldn't afford to buy a Connecticut farm on our editor's and teacher's salaries. We both have family in Maine, so we decided to move north, where the winters are longer but land is cheaper.

Jason made several trips to Maine to interview at a variety of high schools. When he found one that was a good fit, he called a real estate agent and went house shopping the very same day. He found our dream farm on the first try. The next morning I drove up to look at the house—a modest three-bedroom home with a four-car garage and five acres of land in a rural setting, but near a bustling small town—and approved immediately. It was not yet a "horse property," but it was within our price range, and I could easily envision transforming the garage into a barn. After a flurry of paperwork, we signed the papers on our first home. By a stroke of good fortune, we were able to negotiate for grazing rights on the adjoining nine acres of pasture, still owned by the investor who sold us our home. Jason and his father built two 12 x 12 stalls in one side of the four-car garage, we put up electric fencing, and brought George and Beamer to their new home. Since moving north, I've switched from jumping disciplines to focus on dressage and trail riding.

Over the intervening years, we've made many changes and improvements, and it's still not perfect, but our little farm is working for us. We added a run-in shed off the side of the garage so the horses

ABOVE: Jason with Robin and our daughter Isabel.

can live out 24/7, and improved the footing in the sacrifice paddock. We leveled and graded a new section of pasture. We have plans in the works to add two more stalls and a tack room in the barn. George is no longer sound for riding due to an old suspensory injury, so we bought Robin, a 15.1-hand eight-year-old Appaloosa mare, as a trail horse for Jason, and also took in our boarder, Allegro, a 16.3-hand Cleveland Bay/Thoroughbred cross.

Best of all, we were fortunate enough to be able to acquire the thirty-five-acre property directly across the street from our home, which includes a five-acre pasture, an unfinished horse barn and several outbuildings, nearly thirty acres of woodland with existing trails, and mature berry vines and apple trees. We plan to add an arena, to expand the pasture by clearing some of the forest, and either to renovate the existing barn, which is in disrepair, or to build a new one (in which case the old barn will be put to use as a shelter for turkeys, pigs, and goats). Developing this property will be a project to occupy us for decades to come.

LEFT: Beamer and Robin grazing in midsummer at Pleasant Hill Farm.

PART ①

The Farm

1. The Search for a Farm

Location

THERE ARE A lot of factors to consider when looking for your ideal horse farm, and as any real estate agent will tell you, the three most important are location, location, location. As far as property values, the exact same piece of land may vary in price by hundreds of thousands of dollars depending on which state it's in, whether it's in a rural or suburban area, and how desirable its neighborhood is. A five-acre farm with a four-horse barn and three-bedroom home may be priced around $250,000 in a Midwestern state, while a farm with the exact same specifications wouldn't be found for less than $1 million in Westchester or Los Angeles County.

It's likely that your choice of state or region will depend on factors unrelated to your horse farm plans, such as proximity to family and work, so I'll set aside discussion of regional variations and focus on the factors that are the same no matter where you live.

Rural areas are tempting with their lower purchase prices and larger tracts of land, but make sure you consider your family's other needs as well: How far will the commute be to work and school? Do the schools have a good reputation? Are there jobs available in your field? What is the horse community like in the area? Will you have access to lessons, training, social opportunities, and shows in your chosen discipline?

A more suburban area may allow for easier access to urban centers for work, school, cultural, and shopping opportunities, but land is going to be much harder to find and correspondingly much more expensive. In addition, you may have to contend with more regulations and restrictions regarding the zoning and use of your property than in a rural, agricultural area.

Realtors and Other Resources

The Internet has made house-shopping much more user-friendly, but a well qualified real estate agent can be your best friend. Seek out a Realtor with knowledge of horses and horse farms if possible, as these agents will be better able to understand your unique needs and may have leads on horse properties. If not, at least find an agent who specializes in land and farms.

Buy What You Want or Create It?

Generally speaking, it's less expensive in the long run to buy an existing farm with all the amenities you desire, rather than buying

BELOW: A beautiful center-aisle horse barn with well-planned fencing.

land and building your farm from the ground up. Specialized horse facilities such as a barn, fencing, and arena can cost tens of thousands of dollars to build, but these additions are not often reflected equally in the property value. On the other hand, perfect little farmettes are not easy to come by, so if you can't find the horse property of your dreams, you may have to build it.

What to Look For

Important considerations when evaluating any property as a potential farm, whether it's undeveloped land, a house with acreage, or an existing farm, include the following:

Water. Is there a well on the property? Is its size adequate to the needs of your family *and* your livestock? If not, what will be the cost, logistics, and considerations for drilling one? As part of any home inspection, it's important to have well water tested for minerals, contaminants, and bacteria. If water is piped in by the town, as it is in many suburban areas, what will be the cost to you as a homeowner? If there's an existing barn, is water already available in or near the barn and paddock? If not, you will have to either run buried pipes and plumbing to the barn, or resign yourself to lugging buckets and handling hoses daily—in which case, a further consideration is, how far is the house (or nearest outdoor faucet) from the barn? Your property may have some surface water, such as ponds or streams. Keep in mind that you cannot count on using these sources as drinking water for pastured horses, as they may be contaminated or muddy, or may dry up during arid seasons. In fact, environmental protection regulations may specifically require you to fence livestock *out* of areas with surface water.

Topography. Are there existing pastures or open fields, or is the property wooded? Clearing wooded land to create pasture is an expensive and time-consuming proposition; keep in mind that it can cost around $10,000 per acre, and take up to two to three years, to turn virgin forest into usable horse pasture. Is the terrain rolling and hilly, or flat? A flat, open pasture may appear to be ideal, but without hills or a slope, water will have no way to run off, often resulting in standing water or mud in the spring. The best horse pasture has rolling hills to allow water to run off, as well as to help condition the horses as they navigate the terrain. On the other hand, a slope that is *too* steep will break down and erode easily under hoof traffic, and may be unsafe as pasture. Lots of rocks and trees will make mowing a chore, but may provide shade and windbreaks for the horses. Are there wetlands on the property? You won't want to include wetland areas in your pasture plans, since the horses will damage them and cause manure runoff into the water system. If you want to reclaim or alter any wetlands, you may have to get special permission from environmental protection agencies, and in fact you may be restricted from altering them at all.

As you survey the land, keep a sharp eye out for danger zones. Many old farm properties have ancient dumps hidden somewhere in the back forty—a spot where generations of farmers have deposited old rusty barrels, glass bottles, broken farm equipment, old refrigerators and stoves, and even defunct tractors and cars. Obviously, these places are not safe for horses. Even after being cleaned up, there will likely be remnants of rusty metal and sharp broken glass buried under the earth, just waiting to jump out and puncture a sole or sever a tendon. Other dangers might include steep drop-offs, deep bogs, gopher holes, sink holes, barbed wire fence or damaged fencing, and cattle guards.

If no barn currently exists, is there a relatively level spot on high ground near the house where you could build one? Try to visualize the layout of your dream farm on the existing property—where will the barn, sacrifice paddock, run-in shed, and arena be located?

Soil and Pasture Quality. Good soil is a fertile mix of sand, clay, and organic constituents. Soil that is too sandy may not be fertile or stable enough to grow good grass. Soil that has too much clay can be heavy, muddy, and slippery and won't drain well. Overgrazed or damaged pastures may need to be renovated with fertilizer, lime, and reseeding, or may even need to be plowed under, fertilized, and

Rolling, gently hilly terrain is ideal as horse pasture.

replanted with a good horse pasture seed mix. This process is time-consuming and expensive. Count on at least a year of rest before you can graze horses on brand new pasture after plowing and reseeding. Since soil quality can be improved over time, it is not necessarily a deal-breaker when buying property, but it is something to weigh in your mind as you compare potential farms.

Acreage. How many acres do you want? Keep in mind that a ten-acre property does not have ten acres of pasture. At least two acres will be taken up by the house, barn, and surrounding yard. An arena takes up about half an acre. Several other acres may be wooded, steeply sloped, rocky, swampy, or otherwise unusable as pasture. Walk the land yourself, evaluating each part of it as potential horse pasture, to determine exactly how many acres of grazing you will really have. If you plan to use grass as the main forage source for your horses, plan on at least two acres of good-quality pasture per horse, depending on your region's climate. If you manage your farm carefully by practicing rotation grazing, utilizing a sacrifice paddock, and supplementing with hay, you can get away with less. But in an arid climate with sparse grass, you will actually need far more. In some areas of the southwest, the recommended stocking rate is forty acres per head of livestock.

It's advisable—although, I realize, not always affordable—to buy more acreage than you think you will need. When you buy your home, you may have two horses. But, trust me, before long you will be thinking of adding to the herd. Perhaps your daughter is finally old enough for a pony of her own. Perhaps your aging show horse will need to be retired soon, and you want to buy a young one to bring along to replace him. Perhaps you decide to take in a boarder to serve as a companion and to offset some of your costs. Why limit your options with inadequate acreage?

Existing Facilities. Is there a house? Is there a barn? Are they in move-in condition, or will you need to factor extensive renovations into your schedule and budget? Is the barn adequate to your needs? If it's a barn designed for other animals, such as a dairy barn, will you be able to reconfigure it to become a horse barn? Is there an arena, and if so, is it in good condition? If the property is fenced, this is a huge bonus—but is the fencing up to date and in good repair? All of these facilities—barns, arenas, fencing—can be changed or added as needed. But one factor that's very important to most home horse-keepers, and can't necessarily be added if it's not already there, is trail access. Are there riding trails, or at least a wooded area where trails could be developed, on the property? Or are public trails easily accessible nearby? If not, are the local roads safe for riding, with a broad shoulder, minimal traffic, and low speed limit? If you don't have an arena or rideable pasture area, and don't have trail access, you're left with pretty much no options for riding without trailering out each time.

Neighbors. Horse-owning neighbors can be a huge bonus. They will be more understanding of such "nuisances" as whinnying horses, flies, an unsightly manure pile, and early-morning feeding schedules than some other neighbors might be. Horse-friendly, or simply people-friendly, neighbors may be willing to let you ride on their property, or may be willing to exchange vacation horse-feeding responsibilities. Like soil quality, not-so-nice neighbors are not necessarily a deal-breaker—because, like soil quality, they can be improved over time with generous applications of friendly fertilizer (like baked goods and Christmas presents). But neighbors who really dislike horses can make your life miserable, so this is something to take into consideration. If possible, knock on your prospective neighbors' doors and introduce yourself as a potential buyer and

horse owner. Get a sense of their general attitude, and weigh this into your purchasing decisions.

Zoning and Regulations. Is the area zoned for agriculture? Check with the town to make sure it is legal to keep horses and other animals on the property. Make sure you'll be in compliance with any local regulations concerning your horses. For example, many towns have laws limiting the number of horses per acre, or have strict guidelines regarding the disposal of manure or the management of wetlands. If you will be building a barn or other outbuildings, make sure it is possible to get permits, and make sure you'll be able to comply with setbacks and any other regulations *before* you commit to a property.

Taxes and Insurance

In determining your budget for the purchase price of a property, don't forget to include taxes and insurance. Taxes vary greatly by state and by city, so make sure you know what the taxes on your property will be, and make sure you can afford them. Research property insurance, being sure to inform your insurance agent that you will be keeping horses on the property. In many cases they will need to add an extra rider for equine liability coverage. If you will be running any kind of horse-related business on the property, such as boarding, training, or teaching, you will need extra insurance coverage for these activities, and it can be quite expensive. Know what you're getting into before making a commitment.

2. The Barn and Facilities

Barn Design

WHETHER YOU'RE ASSESSING the facilities on an existing property or considering building new structures, there are several factors to take into consideration.

- Distance from the house: How much shoveling will you have to do in the winter? Will you be able to hear or see the horses from the house windows?
- Drainage: The barn or shed should be at the top of a hill rather than the bottom to prevent flooding and mud accumulation outside the doors.
- Angle to the sun: Especially for an open-faced structure like a shed row barn or a three-sided shed, you'll want the open side to face the south and the back to face the north. This allows for maximum sun exposure and minimum wind exposure during the winter.
- Angle to the wind: In hot weather, a breeze blowing through the aisle is a great blessing; in the winter you can shut the doors.

Types of Barns

There are several types of barns to consider, each with its own advantages and disadvantages. The traditional style of barn in New England is the center-aisle barn, with two rows of stalls facing inward

with an aisle down the center. This style of barn allows for a sheltered work and tacking-up area, away from weather and insects. Since the stalls all face one another, it's an efficient work space as well as a beneficial social environment for horses, since they can all see one another easily. The aisle should be at least ten feet wide to allow horses to turn around easily. Another common barn style is the shed row, which is sort of like half of an aisle barn. It's a long shed subdivided into stalls, open in front. This is a popular style of barn in warmer climates, as it allows for better ventilation in the stalls, but may not provide enough shelter in colder climates. There is also no sheltered work area, unless the barn is built with a generous roof overhang in front of the stall doors.

Stalls

In any barn, the minimum standard stall size is 10 x 12 feet, although 12 x 12 is roomier and is my preference for horses taller than 15.2 or so. For ponies, 10 x 10 stalls may be adequate. Larger horses

RIGHT Shed row-style barn with generous overhang to serve as an aisle.

ABOVE: Old New England dairy barn living a second life as a horse barn.

(taller than about 16.2), broodmares with foals, and any horse that will be spending a lot of time in his stall require a larger stall—at least 12 x 14. The stall door should be a minimum of 4 feet wide. Sliding doors are good for saving space in the aisleway and are unbeatable for ease of use. However, they make it impossible to hang anything on the wall where the door slide across, and you can't have a Dutch door that slides. Sliding or swinging stall doors are a matter of personal preference. We built our barn with 12 x 12 stalls and sliding doors.

Stall walls can be made with prefab metal systems that include metal grills along the tops. The builder simply assembles the metal stalls and adds 2 x 4s for the walls. These are beautiful and easy to install, but can be expensive. For our stalls, we used rough-cut hemlock 2 x 6s to assemble a wall frame, and then added hemlock 2 x 10 boards to the outsides. (We chose hemlock because it's inexpensive, yet more durable and harder than pine.) The grills for our stalls are made of hand-welded metal pipes, painted black. We added a layer of ¾-inch plywood to the back walls to serve as kick boards. (That is, if a horse kicks the wall, he will ding the plywood, not the actual wall of the barn. Plywood is also less likely to cause injury to his leg and hoof than solid wood.) I don't like to see solid stall walls to the ceiling in any barn. They don't allow for good ventilation, and they prevent the horses from seeing and interacting with each other, exacerbating a sense of isolation for the stalled horse.

In a wood- or cement-floored barn, rubber stall mats are necessary to protect the horse from the hard surface, as well as to make stall cleaning easier. In fact, stall mats are a boon in any barn, but not strictly necessary in a dirt- or crushed-stone-floored barn. You may find that you want them anyway, since over time the dirt floor will wear away unevenly, requiring additional footing to be added. Make sure the footing in the aisle is durable yet non-slip. Textured concrete or packed dirt works well. Add stall mats down the center of the aisle to create a comfortable, secure working surface that cleans up easily.

In an ideal world, each stall should have a second door at the back for a quick escape in case of a fire. It should be a Dutch door, so you can open the top window in hot weather to increase ventilation in the stall and allow horses to see out. If full doors are not possible, each stall should at least have its own exterior window.

Inside the stall, you'll need horse-safe bucket hangers, wall-mounted salt block holders, stall guards to allow you to work in the stall with the door open, and perhaps hay racks. I don't use hay racks, since it's more natural and healthy for a horse to eat with his head lowered. If you do use them, make sure the bars are finely spaced enough and the rack is hung high enough (about withers height) that a horse won't be able to hang up a hoof in it. I also don't like corner grain buckets that are riveted to the wall, because they're hard to clean. Regular plastic water buckets can become crushed sideways such that they rub on the horse's eyes when he tries to eat, and they

BELOW: Robin in her stall, with a stall guard and sliding door.

RIGHT: Exterior Dutch doors allow the horse to look out, as well as providing emergency access in case of fire.

also break easily. In my experience, the best way to feed grain is at ground level, in a black rubber tub that can be removed, cleaned, and stacked after feeding.

Tack and Feed Rooms

Separate tack and feed rooms are essential for keeping the aisle clean and clutter-free, in keeping with the theory of having "a place for everything and everything in its place." Many people simply use extra stalls as tack and feed rooms, which works well. If space is at a premium, though, the tack and feed areas don't need to be as large as a stall. Ideally, feed should be kept separate from tack, to minimize hay chaff on your expensive leather and to avoid attracting mice to the tack area, which could chew on saddles, pads, wraps, and blankets. Our barn is quite small with limited space for tack and feed, so Jason built a cabinet to store saddles, bridles, and brushes. It lives at the end of the aisle and latches shut to keep dust and hay chaff out.

Make sure your grain bin is secure and rodent-proof. Ours is constructed of heavy-duty plywood, with a hinged lockable top and large plastic storage bins inside for the grain. An old, dead chest freezer is totally rodent-proof and can work very well as a grain bin.

BELOW: A conveniently located and well planned tack room keeps tack clean and accessible.

Shelter

One of the most important aspects of your facility is a run-in shed or lean-to. In order to save hours of time each day and hundreds of dollars each month, you'll want to keep your horses outside as much as possible. To maximize this time and their comfort level, you need a spacious, pleasant, three-sided shelter. This will give them protection from the sun and insects in hot weather, and from wind and precipitation in cold weather. It will give them a dry, clean place to stand during mud season.

Many horse owners simply use their existing stalls, with exterior doors open to the paddocks. This works well with a relatively small number of horses in a stable herd situation, where each horse knows his place in the pecking order and bickering is minimal. If there's a chance that two horses could end up in the same stall and start fighting, it can be dangerous since a stall is so small and it could be hard for the less dominant horse to escape. The benefit to this type of set-up is that it makes feeding a snap. Each horse quickly learns to go into his own stall at feeding time, and you can be sure each horse is getting the right amount and type of grain, supplements, or medications without having to physically lead horses in and out.

BELOW: Our 12 x 30 run-in shed provides enough space to shelter all four of our horses comfortably.

If your barn and pastures are not set up to allow for stall access from the paddock, as mine are not, or if your particular herd dynamics make this option risky, you will need a run-in shed. An ideal run-in shed has several important features:

Size

The shed must be large enough to accommodate all horses that need to use it. Plan on a minimum of 10 x 10 feet of space per horse, but realize that herd disagreements may necessitate dividing the shed or building another if the horses can't all share peacefully. You don't want the low man on the totem pole stuck outside in the blazing sun or driving wind. For more than four or five horses, it may be necessary to maintain separate smaller herds, each with its own run-in shed.

Ceiling and Roof

The shed needs a high ceiling so that horses won't hit their heads if they rear or play inside the shed. The roof should be a minimum of 12 feet high at its lowest point. The roof pitch must be appropriate for weather conditions. Areas that get a lot of snow need a fairly steep pitch to allow the snow to slide off. If the shed is a freestanding structure, the roof should slope toward the back to direct rain and snow away from the opening. Our shed is attached to the side of our barn, so the roof has to slope toward the front. We've had to dig out the soil and add drainage material to the ground along the front to accommodate the increased moisture that accumulates there.

Footing

You'll need level, packed, well-draining footing. The horses will likely be spending quite a bit of time in their shed, and you will need to clean it out daily, just like a stall. A fine gravel packs and drains well, and is easy to clean. I have found that on footing with more organic material or clay, such as native topsoil, manure freezes to

LEFT:
Crushed
gravel
footing is
level and
easy to
clean.

the ground in the winter and is next to impossible to chip off. With crushed stone or gravel, the frozen manure scoops right off. Keep in mind that you will probably need to maintain the footing by topping it off every year or two with fresh material and leveling it again. Using stall mats can eliminate this expense, but then you'll have to bed the shed with shavings to prevent it from becoming slippery, which adds quite a bit more expense itself.

It's somewhat of a personal choice whether or not to use shavings in a run-in shed. Many barn owners don't, arguing that the bedding will encourage horses to use the shed as a "litter box." This may be true, but I do use them in the summer, when the horses spend most of the day in the shed and the pooling urine becomes problematic. I dump a bag onto the area where the horses tend to pee, and leave the rest bare. In winter, I don't use shavings at all, since they freeze solid when wet and are more trouble than they're worth. I stop using them in the fall, when the cooler weather allows the horses to be outside the shed much more and they don't make as much of a mess inside.

Safe Walls and Surroundings

Look for and eliminate any loose nails, broken boards, or sharp edges. Line the lower four feet of the walls with plywood kick boards. There will be multiple horses moving around inside the shed unsupervised, playing and fighting on occasion, which increases the chance of injury if there's anything to get cut or caught on. Minimize the amount of "stuff" in the shed—no hanging buckets, hay racks, or other paraphernalia. A salt block is really all you need to have inside the shed.

To serve as a primary shelter, the shed needs to have three solid walls. Two walls will not provide enough protection from the harsh winter wind. Four walls and a door are not ideal, because an aggressive horse could trap another horse inside and attack him, with no way for the submissive horse to escape. There must be a large, wide opening so that horses can enter and exit safely and easily. We added windows to two sides of our shed, with drop-down panels that we can open in summer and close in winter, adding greatly to the ventilation and comfort level of the horses inside. We also added bright lights, way up in the highest point of the ceiling, well out of range of horse heads. This was a brilliant idea, since I can now check on horses, feed, change blankets, or clean the shed even after sunset, which comes very early in the depths of winter.

BELOW: Robin naps in the sun in the lee of the shed.

Fairwinds Farm

Lilly Golden shares her hundred-acre farm with her husband, two daughters, and five equine friends. Lilly's daughters, fourteen-year-old Isabel and eleven-year-old Rose, are the motivating force behind Lilly's horse passion. Although she rode in lessons and summer camps as a child, from age seven to eighteen, Lilly did not get her first horse until she was forty-two, when her daughters expressed their own interest. "When my two daughters were old enough to ride, we bought our first (naughty) pony and then quickly acquired more horses," Lilly explains. "I restarted my riding career when my daughters began theirs."

The Golden family has four ponies (two of which are retired) as well as Lilly's own horse, 15.3-hand Thoroughbred Luke. The girls' Pony Club mounts are Mojo, a twenty-one-year-old, 13.3-hand, 900-pound tank of an Irish Sport Horse–Welsh Cob cross gelding, and Goldie, a sixteen-year-old Pony of the Americas/Welsh mare (a scant 14 hands), a new member of the herd, replacing Pickle, their beloved twenty-eight-year-old small POA who passed away this summer due to colic. "We were devastated" when Pickle died, recalls Lilly, "and Rose inconsolable. It's terrible to see your child so sad." The two retired ponies are Brownie, a Quarter Horse/Welsh cross mare in her late thirties, retired due to age, and Jenna, their first pony, an eighteen-year-old small Welsh pony retired due to her "very naughty behavior under saddle." Not every small pony makes a good child's pony!

The girls are heavily involved in Pony Club, a well-respected national organization with a focus on eventing and horse care. Lilly trailers Goldie and Mojo to lessons and Pony Club events regularly. One of the few drawbacks to having their ponies at home is the lack of social interaction with other young riders. Pony Club helps fulfill that need. "At home, my girls can only ride with me and with each other, which is wonderful, but they would love to be able to ride to a friend's barn to have other kids to ride

with," Lilly explains. "Unfortunately, we are far from other riders. Pony Club is a wonderful community and they see the members of their Pony Club every few weeks, often with their ponies
in tow during the summer, and without their ponies during the
winter." The biggest challenge for the family is budget. "Trailering to lessons is expensive, but we do as much of it as we can during the summer. At fourteen and eleven years old, the girls are
getting to the point where they would like more than we can provide in the training and competition departments."

The Goldens keep their horses at home out of necessity as
well as desire. In a rural area with no real boarding options, if
they wanted to have horses they would have to be at home. Even
if there were stables nearby, Lilly mentions, "I could not have
afforded the option." In most areas, boarding five horses at a
stable would run somewhere in the range of $2,500 per month.
Horsekeeping at home offers much more flexibility and cost-
effectiveness. In addition to affordability, Lilly appreciates
many of the other benefits of horsekeeping: "The positives are
that you are hands on, always there in an emergency, and always
there for the fun stuff, too. Ninety-nine percent of horse ownership happens on the ground, not while riding. So by having
horses at home, you don't miss any of that 99 percent, including all the hard work of mucking, fence keeping, feeding, loading
hay, breaking ice on winter water troughs, etc. The negatives are
the same as the positives, ironically—the hard work is never done
and it's inescapable."

Fairwinds Farm has a small barn and trails through their
seventy wooded acres, as well as a makeshift arena: "We bull-
dozed a flat area that seems to grow rocks. But we picked (and
continue to pick) those rocks diligently. After the first few years
of rock picking and establishing grass, we were able to begin
using it. Now we ride in it for at least part of every ride and work
on bending, jumping, and dressage. We add field riding and
trails to keep the ponies from getting bored in the ring."

For the most part, the horses live outside and have access to the barn aisle for shelter. Two of the ponies are kept in stalls at night—one because she picks on the other horses, and the other because she's prone to obesity and can't be left on pasture 24/7. Here, Lilly sets a good example of altering your "ideal" horse-keeping practices to take into account the highly individual needs of your horses. While she appreciates her barn and is happy to have it, Lilly says she would have done a few things differently in retrospect: "We built our barn before having enough experience. I would have taken hay loading, manure management, and water access more into account when considering how the barn was built if I had had the advantage of experience." The farm comprises about thirty acres of pasture, but not all of it is fenced, "so they manage to overgraze what I do have fenced in. I could do a lot better with my pasture rotation and management!"

Rose and Isabel are equal partners in this horsekeeping venture. "Sometimes the work elicits groans from the girls, but they love their ponies and are willing to do what it takes to care for them," Lilly says. "They muck and feed their ponies daily. I do not do their chores for them unless there are after-school activities that physically prevent them from being available to do them." The horse chores are part of a lifestyle for Lilly and the girls, one that they wouldn't give up. "The ponies are right here all the time," Lilly points out. "If the girls want to hop on for fifteen minutes bareback, they can. When there are no time constraints they can groom for hours and ride when they're ready. The flexibility is wonderful. During the summer, I ride with them about five days a week. I feel very blessed to be able to share this part of their lives with them."

The ponies are quietly teaching Isabel and Rose some important life lessons. Lilly says of the horses and ponies, "Their delightful personalities are a joy to experience. The act of caring for them is soothing and therapeutic. I love the hard work and that my daughters are learning that hard work bears fruit and that what they love most may take the most effort."

Fencing

There are lots of fencing options for the small-scale horsekeeper, each with its own benefits and drawbacks. The type you choose will depend on the amount of money you can afford to spend, the level of permanence you desire, the type and amount of terrain you're fencing, and the amount of maintenance you're willing to do. Below I've listed some of the more common fencing solutions. While material costs may vary by region, I've provided some general estimates for the purposes of comparison.

Any fence you choose should be 54 to 60 inches in height, with a bottom rail that is 8 to 12 inches off the ground. This height is sufficient to discourage jumping (although stallions or very large horses might require an even higher fence), and the bottom rail is low enough to prevent a horse from trying to graze or roll under the fence while being high enough not to trap a hoof. Fence posts should be sturdy, weather resistant, and driven deeply into the ground. Wood posts should be pressure treated to resist rot. If you choose to use metal T-posts for electric or wire mesh fencing, the tops of the posts must be capped with plastic caps to prevent severe injury. Fencing material should be attached to the inside (horse side) of the fence to prevent horses from pushing the rails off the fence and to provide a smooth, safe interior surface.

A well-constructed and well-maintained wood fence.

Wood Post-and-Rail Fence

A post-and-rail wood fence is the classic choice for horse fencing. It's beautiful, durable, and safe. On the other hand, it's expensive and high-maintenance. For fence lines of any great length, if you don't have a tractor-powered post-hole digger, you'll have to hire someone at least to dig the holes and set the posts. The materials are costly as well. If well constructed, with pressure-treated posts, the fence itself should last many years. However, you'll have to repaint it or restain it every few years, and check the boards and posts often for rot, loose nails, or breaks. One way to extend the life of the fence is to run a single strand of electric tape along the top rail to prevent horses from chewing or leaning on it. The cost to install a new wood fence can vary greatly based on specifications (such as how many rails, what type of wood, whether it's painted/stained or not, and distance between posts) but expect to pay between $8 and $12 per foot of fence line. So, for a one-acre pasture surrounded by 835 feet of fence, the cost will be around $6,680 to $10,020. So it is certainly one of the most expensive options, but on the other hand, nothing beats the eye appeal of a beautiful, classic wood fence.

Electric Fence

Perhaps the most popular type of horse fencing for small-scale horse owners is electric fence. Most horses quickly learn to respect the fence and stay well away from it, so it's very effective. It is relatively easy and fast to put up, and is one of the least expensive options available. You can choose from narrow electric braid fencing, one-inch electric tape, or wider, more visible electric tape. Posts can be wood, steel T-posts, or fiberglass rods, and don't have to be as sturdy or deeply rooted as those intended for a wood fence since the electric tape isn't heavy. I've found the best success with electric braid and a combination of T-posts and fiberglass rods. Tape, as opposed to braided fencing, can stretch over time and its wider surface area makes it much more susceptible to wind damage; on the other hand, it is more visible to the horse. Fiberglass rods alone are not strong enough to hold up a long fence. We use steel T-posts or wood posts at all corners and at least every 40 feet along the fence line, with fiber-glass rods in between for added visibility and to reduce sag. (Note that the T-posts MUST be capped with plastic caps to prevent serious injury. The tops are very sharp, and if a horse tries to jump over, he can injure himself severely.)

Maintenance on a well-installed electric fence is moderate. You'll need to eyeball the fence line regularly to check for downed or broken lines and connectors, and maintain the weeds along the fence line with a combination of mowing, weed-whacking, and herbicides (if you so choose; we don't like to use herbicides on our pastures). Test the fence occasionally with an electric fence tester (or just by touching the line if you're brave!) to make sure the charger is working and that it's not grounded out somewhere. Our electric braid fence has been in place for five years and is holding up quite well. The materials in the fencing do degrade over time, with sun and weather damage, so you will have to replace the tape or braid eventually. Buy the best quality materials you can find, and note the estimated life expectancy of the tape or braid. Some types are considered "temporary" fence and will only last about five years, while top-quality "permanent" fence can last twenty years or longer.

As with any fence, there are some drawbacks to electric fence. The main one is appearance. Electric fence just isn't as nice to look at as wood or vinyl fencing. A poorly maintained electric fence is a sorry sight indeed, with flopping fiberglass posts and sagging, twisted tape. Appreciation for electric fencing seems to be almost a cultural

BELOW: Horses that are happy and content in their pasture are less likely to challenge the fencing.

phenomenon. In some areas of the country, electric fence is denigrated and is not considered to be adequate horse fencing, period. But where I live, in Maine, almost everyone uses it, even top-of-the-line boarding stables. The problem with electric fence is that if it's poorly installed or maintained, it's really bad—a mess to look at, ineffective at keeping horses in, and a maintenance nightmare. If the fence is well installed and well maintained, with top quality materials and a good, strong charger, it's a great fence.

Electric fence is also not a top choice for a small, enclosed area such as a sacrifice paddock, since it's at greater risk for horses running into or through it. Some horses are so afraid of electric fence that they become paralyzed with fear when put into a very small paddock with electric fence. It can also be problematic when used as fencing between two small paddocks with horses in both, as playing or fighting over the fence can destroy it.

On the other hand, electric fence alone may not be adequate for certain horses, such as stallions who may be highly motivated to escape and reach the mares. Some extra-smart and extra-naughty ponies learn to climb through or under the fence, or even run right through it, knowing that it will only hurt for a second. If you own stallions or wily ponies, electric fence may not be the solution you're looking for.

Another perceived disadvantage is the potential for failure of the electric charge. This can happen due to power outages, poor grounding of the fence when initially installed, weeds or snow contacting

BELOW: Keep your electric fence charged to prevent horses from pushing against it.

Dangerous Fencing

There's a lot of terrible fencing out there. Poor fencing is dangerous, as it can injure horses itself (as in the case of uncapped T-posts or broken wooden boards) or allow horses to escape, putting them at risk of being hit by a car or encountering any number of other dangerous situations. Before you bring any horses to your property, assess your fencing for the following conditions, and fix them!

- Loose, broken, or sagging electrical tape
- Too few lines of tape, which would allow a horse to push underneath the top line
- Barbed wire or high-tensile wire
- Rickety, unsecured metal panels
- Rotting wooden posts
- Loose or broken boards
- Boards too close together, which could trap a head or hoof
- Exposed nails
- Uncapped steel T-posts

the fence and grounding it out, or a piece of the line breaking. In my experience, occasional failure of the electric fence is not problematic. If you maintain the fence well and prevent weed contact or breakage, you can easily mitigate that source of problems. When you install your fence, ground it with at least three 6-foot-long grounding rods driven all the way into the ground. Don't skimp on this step—a weak ground makes for a weak fence charge. Similarly, invest in a top-quality charger that will reliably deliver a strong charge. A solar-powered charger circumvents loss of charge due to power outages. During winter when the snow is deep, we only charge the top line, preventing the fence from grounding out when the lower lines are inevitably swallowed up by snow pack. And even in the event that power is lost for some reason, the horses are well accustomed to staying within the fenced area and typically don't try to challenge the fence. The key with any fence is to make sure the horses are happy *inside* the pasture. If they have companions, plenty of room to run, grass or hay to eat, and fresh water to drink, they will be much less likely to try to escape in the first place.

Again, prices will vary for electric fence based on the brand and quality of materials you choose and the number of strands you install, but expect to pay somewhere in the range of 15 cents per foot of fencing, plus the price of a charger (around $100 to $300). So for that same one-acre pasture with 835 feet of fence, you'll pay about $125.

Vinyl or PVC Post-and-Rail Fence

These materials are designed to look like a traditional white wooden post-and-rail fence, but they are made of durable material that won't rot and never needs to be painted. Be sure your fencing is specifically made for horses. There are much cheaper, but much less durable, options available that are made for home use and will break too easily to be used for horses. In addition, make sure your material of choice is treated with a UV protectant to prevent it from becoming brittle and worn due to sun exposure.

Cost is slightly higher than traditional wood fence, at $15 to $18 a foot for a three-rail fence (so about $15,000 for that one-acre pasture), but maintenance is vastly reduced, and the fence will last, essentially, forever.

A similar product is flexible vinyl fencing, which consists of 4- to 5-inch-wide, thin strips of flexible vinyl that provide a visual barrier to the horse. Common brand names of this type of fence are RAMM and Centaur. From a distance they approximate the appearance of a traditional wood fence, but at a much lower cost—about $6 or less per foot for a three-rail fence not including posts, or $5,000 for a one-acre enclosure—and with a longer lifespan. Some varieties are electrifiable for added deterrence. Flexible vinyl fencing may be safer than some other types of fencing, because it doesn't break, yet is flexible, so it won't cut into or bruise horse flesh.

Woven Wire

Woven wire, also called mesh or non-climb, fencing can be ideal for horses. It's made of a matrix of wires woven horizontally and vertically into a loose netlike design. It can be V-mesh, with diamond-shaped spaces, or rectangular spaces. Red Brand is one of the most well-known suppliers of woven wire horse fence. It's very safe, durable, relatively inexpensive, and can contain foals and minis as well as large horses. The only real drawback is that it's not as aesthetically pleasing as traditional post-and-rail fence.

The main concern with woven wire is that you choose fencing that is specifically made for horses, as there are many types of woven wire made for smaller livestock that don't work well for horses. There's a similar product called welded wire that doesn't hold up as well to horse-strength pressure, so be sure you choose woven. In addition, the space between the wires must be 2 inches wide by 4 inches high or less, to prevent horses from getting a hoof between them. The total fence height, as for any horse fence, should be 54 to 60 inches. A nice touch is to add a wooden top rail along the top of the fence to prevent sagging and to provide a finished look.

Posts for woven wire can be wood or steel. Wood is more traditional and durable, while steel T-posts are cheaper. As when using them with electric fence, you must cap the tops of the posts to prevent injury. Cost for woven wire is around $2 to $4 per foot, not including posts.

BELOW: Woven wire adds security to a traditional wood fence in a smaller paddock area.

Just say no to barbed wire fence.

Barbed Wire

Just say no to barbed wire. It's dangerous and unnecessary. Yes, you will hear arguments that ranchers out west have been using barbed wire around their horse pastures for decades and they don't have problems. However, they also have extremely large pastures—we're talking hundreds of acres. The horses aren't going to be right up against the fence the majority of the time. In most backyard or small-scale settings, pastures are one to ten acres at best, and may be subdivided into smaller sections. The risk of a horse trying to escape, being chased through or over a fence by pasturemates, leaning against the fence to get to grass on the other side, or simply brushing up against the fence accidentally is just too great. Horse hide is much more sensitive than that of cows, which are traditionally fenced in barbed wire without incident. Horses are at much greater risk of severe, debilitating injury to their legs or bodies due to the sharp projections on barbed wire fencing. Moreover, horses by nature are more prone to panic than cows when trapped, so a horse that becomes entangled in a barbed wire fence will probably struggle to free himself, causing deep lacerations and wire cuts. It's just not worth the risk. Don't use it.

Arena

A riding arena is a luxury for the home horsekeeper. If you already have one or can afford to have one built, consider yourself lucky! If not, see the section on Making Do in the Handling and Riding chapter for some ideas on riding "outside the box."

Construction

Constructing a riding arena is an art and a science. It requires a profound understanding of drainage, materials, excavation, and the unique footing needs of an arena. Most excavation contractors are very experienced at planning and building roads, foundations, driveways, and parking lots, but only a select few have the knowledge and experience needed for riding arena construction. A poorly constructed arena is heartbreaking: You've just invested tens of thousands of dollars into your dream arena, only to discover that one corner washes away in the first hard rainstorm, the footing is far too deep, and it drains so poorly that it becomes an unrideable swamp for days following each rain. Now you're faced with the choice of suffering with an unsatisfactory arena or investing much more money into repairs to salvage your project.

For these reasons, it's best, as well as most economical in the long run, to seek quotes from contractors who are known to be skilled at arena construction. Ask around to develop a list of local excavation contractors who have built arenas, and then go see some of the arenas they've built. Are their owners happy with how they turned out? Are they holding up well? Was the contractor easy to work with? Did he stay within his quoted budget and schedule?

Another possibility is to do much of the work yourself. This can theoretically save you money, and is feasible if you have the required

BELOW: Riding arena construction underway.

basic excavation knowledge and equipment, *and* if your property has a relatively level, well draining area that would work well for an arena. If you have any standing water or drainage concerns, it's best to bring in a professional.

Considerations when planning your arena include:

Size. Generally speaking, the biggest factor in cost of an outdoor arena is size (although sites that need heavy excavating or require a lot of base material will cost more regardless of size). There is some variation in cost for different types of footing, but for the most part the most effective way to minimize cost is to limit size. If you must cut costs, build a smaller arena, not a bigger arena with sub-standard construction.

To some extent, the size of your arena will also depend on your discipline. A standard small dressage arena is about the minimum size for almost any riding discipline. At 20 meters (66 feet) wide, it is wide enough to allow the horse to canter with ease. A narrower width will result in turns that are too tight to be comfortable for the horse. For jumping, a larger, wider arena—about 150 by 200 feet wide— is preferable. You can work within the confines of a large dressage arena, but a small dressage arena will be too limiting. Reining, barrel racing, and disciplines that involve working cows require arena space of about 150 feet by 260 feet. A round pen should be at least 50 feet in diameter, although 60 feet is even better and will allow you to do a bit of riding in it as well as just lunging and groundwork.

Location. Choose a high spot to minimize drainage problems. A lower spot on the land will introduce runoff problems as rain runs downhill onto and through the arena. The arena should also be fairly close

Arena Size

Dressage (small)	66 x 132 feet
Dressage (large)	66 x 196 feet
Jumping	150 x 200 feet
Reining/Barrel racing	150 x 260 feet
Working cows	150 x 260 feet
Round pen	60 feet in diameter

A riding arena is a major advantage for disciplines that involve jumping.

to the barn and house for convenience as well as proximity to phones and access to emergency vehicles in case of an accident. This will also help herd-bound horses focus on their work instead of worrying about their friends. Proximity to the road, or at least a good access driveway, is important both for construction equipment and dump trucks during construction, and for bringing in new material as the arena ages.

Type of footing. It's important to know what your goals are for your arena footing. Different disciplines have different requirements as far as traction, depth, and so on. Choices for footing also vary based on climate, dust management, or other maintenance concerns, as well as cost. There are a lot of options to choose from, so it's critical to know what your main objective is. This approach helps to narrow down your field of options and ultimately time and cost. Options range from a simple sand arena to a high-tech specialized footing material made of rubber, leather, or engineered polymers. Your contractor should know what options are available and should be able to help you choose a footing material that suits your specific needs.

Depth of footing. Like footing material, the depth of footing is, to some extent, a personal choice based on discipline and type of footing material. Very deep footing is not safe for horses to work in, as it can lead to soft tissue injuries. For the most part, a depth of two to four inches is ideal for most purposes. As a rule of thumb, it's

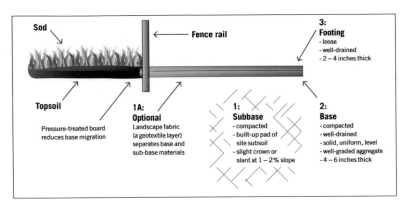

ABOVE: The footing is the top layer of a multilayered system. A chain is only as strong as its weakest link, and an arena is only as good as its base.

better to have too little footing than too much. It's always possible to add more footing after working in it for a while, but it's much harder to remove existing footing if it turns out to be too deep. If too much footing has been delivered, just keep it in a pile under a tarp at one end of the arena, to be added as needed over time.

Fencing. A three-rail white-painted wooden fence is the traditional enclosure for a riding arena. Place the rails on the inside of the posts to avoid catching a toe on a fencepost as you trot by. Metal pipe panels can also work well, although they are less visually appealing. A true dressage show arena does not have a fence at all—only a low chain or rope as a visual barrier—but for your personal purposes you may find a fence useful. It will keep your horse contained in case of any unplanned dismounts, spooks, or bolts, as well as keeping children and other animals out. *Never* use electric fence or any type of wire as an enclosure around a riding arena, as it is unsafe.

Proximity to power and water. You may want to install arena lighting. This will allow you to use your arena before and after work hours even during the darker times of year. Remember that for much of the year, it is dark by 5 PM, which severely cuts into your riding time if you don't have lights. So, where is the closest power source to your arena? Will you be able to set up lights without running expensive underground lines for a long distance? In addition, many types of arena footing require frequent watering to prevent them from becoming dusty during dry seasons. How close is the nearest hose faucet? Can you run a buried water line right to the arena?

Maintenance

Once your arena is complete, your work is not yet done. To keep your arena pleasant and rideable, you'll have some new chores to do. Each time you ride, pick up any horse manure that's left behind. Old, dried-up, pulverized manure will mix with the footing and change its consistency over time, making it powdery and dusty. Many types of footing, especially sand, need to be watered regularly to prevent dust and compaction. Use a lawn sprinkler attached to a garden hose to water the arena as needed.

The arena will need to be dragged periodically to smooth out ruts as well as to "fluff up" the footing and prevent it from compacting over time. Frequency depends on how heavily the arena is used. Commercial stables may drag their arenas daily; you might get away with dragging once or twice a month. You can use an ATV or lawn tractor pulling a simple chain drag, or even a weighted box spring if you don't mind looking a little redneck, for this purpose. However, these types of drags will only address the top inch or two of the footing, so over time a compacted base may form under the top layer. To prevent this, look for a specialized drag with flexible, V-point spring tines that will dig deep into the footing. Be sure that your drag is not cutting into the base material.

Finally, even with routine dragging your arena may develop low spots, especially a rut along the rail where the most traffic occurs. You may also see buildup of footing materials in the corners where the drag can't reach. When this occurs, you'll have to hand-rake the arena to move the footing material from the high spots to the low spots.

Trails

If you're lucky enough to have trails on your property, they'll need some maintenance as well. Well established trails will just need to be trimmed up a bit every spring—go through with a machete or pole saw and remove any low-hanging branches or limbs that have sagged or fallen into the path. Remember, if you're walking, that your head will be about four feet higher when you're mounted on a horse, so clear branches as high as you can reach.

Wet areas can be improved somewhat with the addition of fill or wood chips, although a very wet spot such as a small stream crossing may require placing a culvert to allow the water to pass through. Clear, open water is better left alone, both to avoid messing too much with the ecosystem and to provide an excellent training opportunity for water crossings.

Assess the footing on the trail and look for hazards such as rocks, roots, or other obstacles protruding from the soil. Large rocks and roots are very hard to remove and will leave a big hole, so it's better to leave them as is and spray-paint them orange or white for high visibility. Remove anything that's sharp or stabby-looking.

In the case of relatively new or soft trails, one of the best steps you can take to keep them in good shape is to avoid using them when it's very wet or muddy. Heavy use during these periods can do irreparable damage.

3. Management and Maintenance of Facilities

Equipment

EVERY HORSE FARM needs certain fundamental pieces of equipment. Most of these are self-explanatory, so here I'll just offer a series of lists as inspiration. The three "big ticket" items, tractors, trucks, and trailers, are discussed in their own separate sections below.

Grooming kit. Hard and soft brushes, curry, mane and tail comb, hoof picks, scissors, fly spray, detangling spray, bath sponges, bath bucket, shampoo, sweat scraper, shedding blade, towels, clippers, braiding kit if needed. Ideally, keep a separate kit of basic brushes for each horse to avoid cross-contamination of contagious skin conditions.

Equine first aid kit. Bag Balm, antibiotic wound ointment, icthammol, Epsom salts, VetWrap, roll cotton, non-stick wound pads, standing bandages, poultice,

English tack.

iodine scrub, scissors, Banamine, Bute, latex medical gloves, twitch, thermometer, weight tape, list of each horse's normal vital signs.

Barn cleaning tools. Wheelbarrow, manure forks, broom, rake, muck buckets, scoop shovel, bucket scrubbers.

Tack. Saddles, bridles, girths, martingales, boots, polo wraps, bell boots, a variety of bits, saddle pads, halters and lead ropes, whips or crops, lunge line, lungeing cavesson, lungeing surcingle and side reins. Choices in tack are highly individual depending on discipline and personal preference, and you may need more or fewer items than those listed here.

Boots and wraps. Bell boots, galloping boots, polo wraps, standing wraps, pillow wraps.

Horse clothing. Turnout blankets, stable blankets, turnout sheets, dress sheets, fly sheets and masks, fleece or wool coolers, quarter sheets, shipping wraps.

Feeding equipment. Buckets, grain feeders (stall-mounted or flat pans on the ground), measuring scoops, scale for weighing grain and hay, scissors to cut hay string, hay nets, large water trough, heated buckets, water tank de-icer, rodent-proof containers for grain storage, pallets for short-term hay storage.

Things Without Which I Could Not Live

Water bucket heater and/or heated buckets

Tractor

Wheelbarrow

Hoses—don't forget to drain them!

Latex medical gloves

Run-in shed

Bag Balm

Tractor

Do you need a tractor? Not necessarily. Many small horse farms function quite well without a tractor, and you can get by without one. However, a tractor is an extremely useful and versatile piece of farm equipment, and makes many tasks easier and quicker. A rule of thumb is that a farm of ten acres or more needs a tractor, while one less than ten acres does not, but there are many more variables, including how many horses there are, what kind of maintenance the pastures and paddocks need, how physically fit and able-bodied are the people doing the work, and more. Another consideration is the cost. A tractor is extremely expensive, even if you buy used, ranging from $6,000 to $25,000 for a compact utility model, which is the best choice for a small horse farm. Then the implements, such as a loader, bush hog, hay spear, backhoe, or grader all represent considerable additional expense. You will need to make your own assessment as to whether a tractor fits within your budget and is necessary for your farm. When it comes time to purchase a tractor, visit a local dealership and explain your needs and intended uses to the salesperson. Tractor dealers tend to be knowledgeable and helpful, and will work with you to select the ideal size, make and model, and attachments to suit your needs and budget.

Some of the horse-related tasks for which we use our tractor regularly include:

- Mowing pastures with the bush hog attachment
- Digging out rocks and stumps with the backhoe attachment

- Turning the manure pile with the backhoe
- Scooping and moving piles of manure with the loader
- Adding and grading footing with the loader
- Digging fence post holes with a post-hole digger attachment
- Carrying full 70-gallon water troughs to remote pastures in the loader

In addition, we use our tractor for many other farm tasks that don't relate directly to the horses. For example, my husband produces and sells firewood from our thirty acres of wooded land, killing two birds with one stone by gradually clearing the land for a future arena and expanded pasture space. The tractor and its implements are used in every step of this process, from dragging felled trees out of the woods to splitting logs with a power take-off (PTO)-driven wood splitter and moving split wood in the bucket loader.

When purchasing a tractor, one of the important considerations is which implements or attachments to choose. On most horse farms, the two attachments that are used the most are the bush hog or mower and the bucket loader. The bush hog is a rotary mower attached to the tractor's PTO that cuts and mulches grass and is powerful enough to blast through tall weeds and even shrubbery. With a wider mowing base than any lawn mower, it will speed up the work as well.

BELOW: Bush-hogging a pasture with a small tractor.

The bucket loader is an integral part of your machine. Although it's technically an attachment, I would almost say there's no point to having a small farm tractor without a loader. It's versatile and can be used for scraping, scooping, lifting, dumping, spreading, and grading material as well as, in a pinch, plowing snow. You can use it to back-drag the accumulated layer of manure and hay chaff from your paddock in the spring, scoop it out, move it to the manure pile, and then dump in new gravel, spread it, and grade it, all with the bucket

Tractor Implements

Attachment	Function
Backhoe	Digging large holes; rock and stump removal; turning manure pile; digging trenches for irrigation, drainage, or power or water lines
Bale spear	Large tine used for moving round bales of hay
Blade	Grading; snow removal
Box scraper	Grading the footing in paddocks, arenas, round pens
Bucket (loader)	Moving, lifting, dumping, or grading materials such as dirt, sand, manure, hay bales, bedding, snow
Bush hog	Mowing pastures
Chain harrow	Dragging arenas and pastures
Manure spreader	Spreading composted manure on fields
Post hole digger (auger)	Digging holes for fence posts
Rock rake	Removing rocks from loose soil; grading
Snow blower	Snow removal
Tiller or disk harrow	Tilling pastures and arenas

loader. Several other attachments can be very useful on a horse farm. These are listed in the chart on page 55. Carefully consider the chores that you will be doing most frequently on your farm, and purchase implements accordingly.

Truck

On most small farms, a truck is used to purchase larger quantities of hay, shavings, and grain. On the other hand, many feed stores will deliver grain and shavings (albeit for an additional cost), and your hay supplier may also be willing to deliver if you have storage space for a large load. The other major benefit of a truck is that it allows you to have a horse trailer. For general farm use, any old truck will do; it doesn't have to be fancy or brand-new. But if you're going to be hauling a trailer, you need a truck that's in good condition so you're not left stranded by a breakdown with a trailerload of horses. A tow vehicle needs to be four-wheel-drive and at least ¾ ton, depending on the size and weight of the trailer and horses to be towed. Make sure you buy a truck with a tow package, or can have one installed after purchase. Never try to haul with an SUV or other smaller vehicle, even if it seems to pull the trailer easily, as the braking capacity and wheelbase are not adequate to ensure safety.

Trailer

You don't *need* a trailer . . . but then again, you don't *need* horses either, do you? Owning a trailer will increase the amount of fun

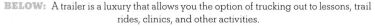

BELOW: A trailer is a luxury that allows you the option of trucking out to lessons, trail rides, clinics, and other activities.

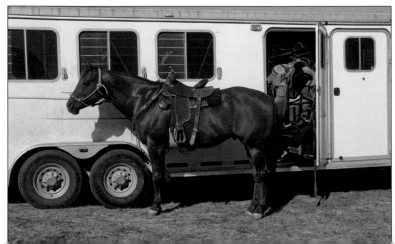

you're able to have with your horses by making it convenient for you to travel to clinics, shows, lessons, and trail riding destinations. It's also an important safety precaution. When a horse suffers from a life-threatening or difficult-to-diagnose illness, he may need to be trailered to an equine hospital, often under emergency conditions. It's best to have your own trailer ready to roll, rather than having to scramble and call friends and neighbors in a panic trying to track down someone with a truck and trailer that you can use.

Considerations for buying a trailer:

Size: Do you need a two-, three-, or four-horse trailer? To me there's not a lot of point in having a one-horse trailer, since it will limit your options so severely—you won't be able to bring a friend along on a trail ride or to a show, for example. Consider what your uses for the trailer will be, and select accordingly. Most small farms are just fine with a two-horse model. Make sure the interior dimensions are large enough to accommodate your horses. A two-horse straight-load trailer intended for full-size horses (as opposed to ponies) should be at least 6 feet wide and 7 feet tall inside.

Gooseneck or bumper pull: Goosenecks are more stable, easier to haul, and provide extra storage space in the gooseneck, but they require a bed hitch in your truck. They are also more expensive than the traditional bumper-pull trailer.

Straight load or slant load: Straight-load trailers have two side-by-side "stalls," and the horses walk straight into the trailer and stand facing forward. In a slant-load trailer, the horses stand at an angle to the direction of travel. Most two-horse trailers are straight-load, while most three-horse trailers are slant-load. Larger trailers with capacity for four or more horses may be straight-load head-to-head or slant-load style. If you have very large horses, you may find that you're better off with a straight load, since the dimensions of a slant-load are necessarily limited by the width of the road. Another drawback to a slant-load is that unless there's an escape door at the front, the horses located at the front of the trailer are trapped in the event of an emergency if the horse at the back can't be unloaded for any reason. There is much debate over whether it's more comfortable

LEFT: Bumper-pull straight-load two-horse trailers.

RIGHT: In this gooseneck slant-load trailer, horses can look out the side windows while the trailer is parked. (Always close the windows before heading down the road.)

for horses to travel straight or at a slant, but it ultimately comes down to personal preference as well as practicality.

Stock trailer or horse trailer: Benefits of a stock trailer—an open-walled design with one or more loose box stalls rather than individual tie stalls—are increased ventilation, decreased purchase price, and the ability for horses to travel loose, which some believe is better for them. Drawbacks are that they are very cold in winter due to the open construction, they may tend to be less well constructed and have fewer perks (such as a tack room) depending on the brand, and you have to be sure to buy one that's an appropriate size and height for horses rather than cows or smaller livestock. Some stock trailers come with a conversion kit that allows you to divide the open box into two straight-load stalls.

Ramp or step-up: Some trailers have a wide, sturdy drop-down ramp at the back, while others simply drop off, requiring horses to step up into the trailer and jump off to unload. Ramp-load trailers seem to be easier for horses to navigate, but most have no trouble learning how to hop in and out of a step-up, so this is another matter that comes down to personal preference.

Tack storage, dressing room, living quarters, and other extras: It's a real benefit to have a dedicated space for your tack in the trailer. Otherwise you'll have to stuff it into the backseat or bed of the truck, where it takes up needed space and may be exposed to the elements. If the trailer includes a large enough tack area to also serve as a dressing room, more's the better. Of course, each of these elements adds to the purchase price, but you will likely find the increased cost to be well justified by the benefits. If you really want to up the ante and plan to spend a lot of time camping or showing at overnight venues, a living-quarters trailer may be just the thing for you. If you're going to go this route, I'd recommend working through a horse-trailer dealer who can help you navigate the available options, rather than buying used through classified ads or online.

Pasture Management

One of the most important, and time-consuming, aspects of horse care is good pasture management. When I decided to buy a farm, after boarding at stables with dirt paddocks, it was crucially important to me that my horses have access to grass as much as possible. It's healthier and more natural for horses to graze freely on fresh, green grass than to be fed hay or concentrates, and I think it's important for their mental health as well. However, keeping your pastures healthy and productive takes some planning and some effort.

Rotation

Pasture rotation is key. If horses have access to all the grass all the time, they will eat the good grass down to nothing and the weeds will begin to take over. The grass will never have a chance to recover

BELOW: Three of our pastures in late summer. The middle one is visibly eaten down, and the horses have just been moved off it.

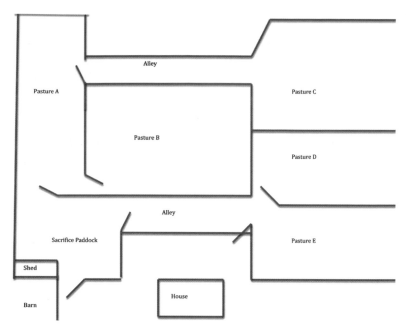

ABOVE: The fencing design at Pleasant Hill Farm allows access to all pastures from the sacrifice paddock.

and grow. The solution is to cross-fence your acreage with multiple pastures, and rotate the horses into a fresh pasture every few weeks. Meanwhile, you can mow, drag, fertilize, or seed the other pastures as needed. Even if you use wood or another more permanent style of fence for your perimeter, there's no reason not to use less expensive and more portable electric fencing for the cross-fencing.

This scenario does present a couple of practical challenges. If the pastures are spread far apart and far from your water source, how will you supply water to each pasture in a convenient way? If your horses use a run-in shed, will you have to build a separate shed in each pasture? If not, are you available and willing to bring them in if they start running from the horseflies or if a sudden thunderstorm blows up? These technicalities can be prohibitive for your pasture management scheme, so be sure to plan your pasture layout carefully.

Our solution, after much trial and error, was to design our pastures such that each can be reached from the sacrifice paddock (a dry lot) via a series of gates and alleys. Our paddock is right next to the barn, and is our main means of access to the horses for feeding and care. Water is easily available, so we keep two large troughs filled, and their large run-in shed is in the paddock as well. We rotate pastures simply by opening and closing the gates to allow the horses into whichever pasture we choose. (See diagram on previous page.)

The bonus to this setup is that it takes advantage of the horse's natural desire to roam. The horses must walk back and forth from the grass pastures to the dirt paddock whenever they need shelter or water, or when they hear us calling them in for meals. The result of all this movement is that the horses all naturally maintain a base level of fitness that horses on regular pastures might not have. In our case, the effect is amplified by the fact that the paddock is at the top of a hill, so they have to go up and down the hill multiple times a day, an activity that is known to be excellent for building athletic fitness and muscle tone in the back and hindquarters.

Sacrifice Area

A well-planned sacrifice area is a must. This is a fenced paddock that you can use for turnout during times when the horses can't be on the pastures. You do not expect to grow grass in this area—it will be bare dirt. Keep horses gated in the paddock whenever the pastures are sensitive—during heavy rains that create muddy conditions, in early spring when the grass is just starting to grow, and late fall or winter when there's no snow cover yet but the grass has stopped growing. Allowing horses onto the grass pastures during these times would be destructive to your delicate grass ecosystem. You can also use a sacrifice paddock if you don't have enough acreage to support all your horses. Keep them in the sacrifice area for several hours a day and provide hay, and let them onto the grass only for short periods. This will allow you to maintain at least some grazing access without destroying your whole property. You can also use it to isolate a specific horse from the grass for dietary reasons, such as an overweight, laminitic, or insulin resistant horse, without having to resort to a stall.

The sacrifice paddock is an integral part of my rotation grazing system, outlined above. The run-in shed and water troughs are

Allegro, Robin, and Beamer napping in their sacrifice paddock.

located at the central sacrifice area, where the horses will spend the most concentrated amount of time. They have access to any of the grass pastures from this paddock, depending on which gates we choose to open.

Choose the location for your sacrifice area carefully. You want it to be close to the barn, house, and water sources for convenience and easy access. Make sure the gate is wide enough to drive a truck or tractor through for maintenance purposes. It should be located on high ground to maximize drainage and minimize mud; situate your run-in shed at the highest point within the paddock if there is a slope to the land. Never locate a sacrifice area near streams, ponds, swamps, or wetlands. This is to prevent contamination of the water supply by runoff manure as well as to keep the area as dry and mud-free as possible. If your native soil is fairly organic or heavy with clay, you will benefit from removing the topsoil and replacing it with gravel or crushed stone, which drains better, helps prevent mud, packs hard for easy manure removal and maintenance, and is abrasive and beneficial for hoof health. Adding a layer of geotextile fabric between the subsoil and the gravel will add stability and prevent the two from mixing together.

The size of a sacrifice area can vary depending on your needs and the number of horses using it. At minimum, it can be a small 12 x 24 paddock attached to a single stall, to be used by one horse. I would not keep a horse long-term in this small of an area, but it's fine for short-term use, allowing the horse access to fresh air and a bit of exercise. If the paddock is going to be used heavily for multiple horses, it should be much bigger, to allow freedom of movement for exercise and play. As a rule of thumb, a minimum length of 100 feet allows horses to trot comfortably, while a minimum of 200 feet allows them to canter and gallop.

Plan to keep your sacrifice area relatively clean of manure and organic matter, such as leftover hay, by picking it regularly. Left unattended, manure and old hay will build up and create a muddy, smelly mess that is unhealthy for hooves and legs. Winter can be problematic, as snow can quickly cover the manure before you have a chance to clean it off, and the result is a sloppy mess in the spring. Try to keep at least a small area near the shed clear of snow and clean of manure, and plan to bring in a tractor to clean up the rest in the spring.

Mowing

Even if your horses keep the grass eaten down pretty well, you'll still have to mow every few weeks. One major reason for this is weeds. Horses won't—and shouldn't—eat most weeds that may grow in the pasture, such as milkweed, buttercups, burdocks, and goldenrod. Left unattended, these weeds will quickly grow out of control and start to take over your lovely grass pastures. Fortunately, mowing helps not only to cut down the weeds but to abbreviate their reproductive cycle and prevent them from spreading. Grasses evolved to survive and thrive under pressure from browsing animals, so mowing is actually beneficial to the grass. But if you mow down the weeds before they have a chance to go to seed, you can limit their spread and hopefully even eliminate them over time. Mowing also results in a more palatable and nutritious pasture, as tall, mature grasses are tougher for the horses to eat and are lower in nutrients.

You will also discover that the horses will not eat grass that is anywhere near, or may at some time in the recent past have been near, any manure. (This phenomenon is known to biologists as the "zone of repugnance"—a fit-

RIGHT: Regular mowing reduces weeds while encouraging grass growth.

ting title.) So to keep the pasture looking even, you'll have to mow. Mowing also exposes manure to the sun, allowing it to dry out and preventing the spread of parasites. We rotate our pastures, and mow right after the horses have been moved off a given section of pasture. This knocks back the weeds and allows the manure to dry out and degrade while the grass has a few weeks to regrow before the horses move back onto it.

You can use a regular lawn mower to mow your pastures, but depending on how much acreage you have, it may take a prohibitively long time to do so (especially if you have a push mower!). In addition, most lawn mowers don't have a high enough blade setting for pastures. You want to mow at about 4 inches, both to avoid scalping the pasture and to protect your mower blades from any errant rocks. It's better and far more efficient to use a bush hog attachment for your tractor. After mowing, you may want to drag the pastures with a rake or harrow to break up manure clods and spread them evenly.

Fertilizing, Liming, and Seeding

Over time, the soil fertility of a pasture is depleted as nutrients are removed (by grazing horses) and not replenished. Therefore, pastures need to be fertilized one or two times a year for optimal production. Signs of a depleted pasture are slow-growing grass, a yellow or light green color instead of dark green, reduced winter hardiness, and reduced stalk strength. To remedy these problems, a mixture of nitrogen, phosphorus, and potassium is needed.

BELOW: At first glance, this pasture appears to be lush. But a closer look reveals that it's sparse and weedy, in need of mowing, fertilizer, and re-seeding.

One way to do this is simply to spread composted horse manure over the pastures with a manure spreader. This is beneficial in the sense that it helps solve the problem of what to do with all that manure, and there is a certain cyclical harmony to it as well. Better yet, it's free and it's organic. However, there are a couple of drawbacks—if the manure has not been adequately composted, there may be remaining parasite eggs that can be re-ingested by the horses when they return to the pasture. In addition, inadequately composted and aged horse manure may be too "hot," meaning it is too high in nitrogen, and can actually be harmful to the grass. Finally, although some nutrients will certainly be returned to the soil, it may not be enough and the balance may not be correct.

It's best to start by performing a soil test. Contact your local agricultural extension service for details on how to do this. They may have instructions or even a kit for gathering a soil sample, which they can test for you. With the results of the soil test, they will advise you as to the best course of action for adding fertilizers to your soil.

Fertilize in the fall, when the ground is hard and dry, or in the early spring before it has gotten too muddy. For best absorption of nitrogen, it's best to time your application of fertilizer the day before a rain shower. Remove the horses from the pasture and mow it before fertilizing. Do not return the horses to that pasture until it has been thoroughly drenched with rain to wash the nutrients off the grass and down into the soil.

Another aspect of soil fertility is acidity, or soil pH. Highly acidic soil reduces plants' ability to absorb phosphorus and micro-nutrients, as well as inhibiting nitrogen-fixing microorganisms. Your soil analysis will report your soil's pH level. The ideal level is between 5.5 and 6.8. If your soil's pH is too low (that is, the soil is too acidic) you can amend it by adding lime or calcium carbonate. Again, your agricultural extension service should be able to advise you regarding how much lime to apply given your specific soil analysis results.

If a pasture has been heavily overgrazed or severely depleted, it may need to be renovated. After fertilizing and liming to optimal levels, overseed with a good quality horse pasture mix that's well suited to your growing environment. Overseeding simply means drilling or broadcasting seed over an existing pasture without first tilling the soil. For a truly derelict pasture or a brand-new pasture, you'll need to till, aerate, and level the soil before drilling or broadcasting seed. It's likely that as a small-scale horse farmer, you don't have all the required equipment for this process. Ask around and hire a local hay grower or other crop farmer who can do the job for you with the right tractor attachments. Again, your agricultural extension service is the best source for information and resources on selecting a seed blend and hiring a farmer.

Manure Management

According to Benjamin Franklin, the only two certainties in this world are death and taxes. To this I would add horse manure. Horses produce a simply astonishing amount of waste, and you will need to have a plan for how to deal with it. Stalls must be cleaned daily, and run-in sheds and sacrifice paddocks also need daily picking to prevent an unhealthy buildup of manure and urine. Each year, the average horse can produce eight to ten *tons* of horse manure, or fifty to seventy pounds per day.

In a suburban area with very limited acreage, your best bet may be to contract with a waste removal company that can provide a dumpster and haul away the contents when it's full. This minimizes smell and mess in the short term (which is very important when you have neighbors in close proximity), and saves a lot of labor in the long term. Try to find a spot for the dumpster that is close to the road for easy access by the removal truck, and is in a low area next to a hill so you can push your wheelbarrow up the hill and dump it down into the dumpster. Otherwise you'll have to use a ramp, which is difficult and can be dangerous, especially in wet or icy conditions. (Another option is to use your tractor bucket to lift and dump the manure into the dumpster.) Drawbacks to this system are expense and the fact that it's not very environmentally friendly.

Another option that's relatively low labor is to build one large manure pile and either pay or beg someone to haul it all away periodically. You'll need to have a spot for the pile that's close enough to the barn to be convenient, but far enough that the smell and flies won't be as problematic. You also need to consider runoff problems and unsightliness. This is another less-than-ideal scenario, for the above reasons.

The best way to handle the manure question is composting. That large pile referenced above will compost on its own over time, but it's faster and more effective to use smaller piles that can be turned by hand or with a tractor. Maintain three smallish piles—one fresh one to which you are actively adding manure, one that is in the process of aging, and one that contains finished compost ready for use as fertilizer in your garden or on your pastures. Situate your manure piles in a place where water runoff will be least problematic (that is, away from wetlands and wells), that is easy to access by wheelbarrow for dumping, and that is easy to access by tractor for turning and removal. A really excellent idea would be to build three open-front concrete bunkers into a hillside. You can push your wheelbarrow up the back of the hill and dump the contents down into the bunker easily, while a tractor can drive around to the front of the hill and access the openings. You can add any other organic waste material to your piles, including lawn clippings, leaves, or kitchen scraps. Never add meat or cat or dog waste to a compost pile.

A compost pile will get very hot as microorganisms break down the organic matter. This heat is a good test of whether your compost pile is working well. A compost thermometer can help you assess the temperature of your pile, which should rise to 135 to 160°F over a period of weeks, then stabilize at that temperature for several days before gradually reducing to the ambient temperature. To achieve high enough composting temperatures to kill parasites, bacteria, and weed seeds, a pile must be at least three or four feet high. Otherwise, the heat generated in the initial stages will quickly dissipate before the pile can reach high enough temperatures. If the temperature is too high (above 160°F), your pile may be too large.

Benefits of Composting

- Reduced smell
- Reduced fly-breeding environment
- 50 percent reduction in volume of material
- Turns a waste product into a useful fertilizer
- Heat kills parasites, weed seeds, and bacteria

Keep the piles moist, but not too wet. The material on the inside of the pile should feel damp, like a wrung-out sponge. Dripping wet is too wet, while crumbly material is too dry. You may want to cover the piles with a tarp to minimize runoff and saturation when it rains. Turn the piles every few weeks to add oxygen and move the outermost material to the inner part of the pile where composting occurs. If the piles are too dry, add water with a garden hose while turning. During summer, a well-maintained pile will complete the composting process in one to two months. During winter, when colder temperatures slow down the process, it may take three to six months. Over the course of time, the pile will reduce in size by 50 percent.

The result will be a soft, dark, pleasant-smelling soil-like product called humus that is ideal for use in flower or vegetable gardens or on pastures. This composted product is much more marketable to local farmers or gardeners than fresh, uncomposted manure and bedding. If you're lucky, you may be able to find people who are willing to actually pay for your compost. Otherwise, people may be interested in hauling it away for free to use as fertilizer. Mushrooms and garlic, in particular, require large amounts of composted horse manure to grow well.

Mud Management

Mud may seem like an inevitable side effect of keeping horses, especially when acreage is limited. Horses quickly eat and destroy foliage that stabilizes the soil, and their hard, heavy hooves are extremely destructive to the remaining earth. On top of that, their manure adds organic materials to the soil, causing it to hold in moisture. Without attentive management, they can and will turn their pastures into mucky swamps. Mud is not good for horses, for a variety of reasons. It makes chores more difficult for their caretaker, for one thing—pushing a wheelbarrow through a soupy mess is nearly impossible; deep mud is hard even to walk through without losing a boot; and grooming is a nightmare every time. More importantly, mud is detrimental to the health of horses. It harbors bacteria and fungi that can infect the hooves and the skin of the lower legs, and constant exposure to moisture is detrimental to the hoof wall. Feeding hay on top of mud (inevitably mixed with manure) contributes to parasite infestation, as horses inadvertently re-ingest the worm eggs found in manure.

The good news is that you can minimize, if not completely eliminate, mud by following two simple rules: 1. Maintain a sacrifice area with good, well draining footing on high ground, and 2. Prevent horses from accessing grass pastures when they are saturated during and after a rain or in the spring.

As long as you've followed step 1, step 2 should be easy. Just provide your horses with hay in the sacrifice area, and close the gates to the pastures anytime it rains. I close off my pastures for several weeks

BELOW: Spring in a wet climate leads inevitably to mud—unless you take proactive steps to protect your pastures.

in the early spring, when snowmelt and rain combine to saturate the ground and the delicate young grass shoots are just starting to grow.

Step 1 is more difficult to put into practice, but once you have established your sacrifice area, it is easy to clean and maintain. See the discussion of sacrifice areas above for details on how to locate, plan, and build a sacrifice paddock. In terms of mud management, the most important details are drainage, footing, and keeping the paddock clean and free of manure. You'll need to replace the native soil with gravel, coarse sand, or crushed stone in your sacrifice area as well as any high-traffic areas such as gates and water troughs. Be sure to choose material that is less than ¾ inch in diameter, or less if possible. A larger size is uncomfortable for horses to stand on, and is harder to clean, as the stones will get caught in the tines of your pitchfork. If you're unsure of what to ask for, or what's available in your area, ask the friendly folks at the gravel pit for a material that packs, drains, and is a maximum of ¼ to ¾ inch in diameter.

My paddock is located at the top of a long, sloping hill, and naturally drains fairly well as a result. Even so, in spring and at rainy times, it often became a sea of mud for days or weeks at a time. After three years of this, we finally got smart. We used a tractor to scrape off the layer of topsoil and manure, and replaced it with 4 inches of primary sand, which is a mixture of coarse sand and ¼-inch crushed gravel. This material packed down into a hard, level, well-draining surface that is easy to keep clean and resists becoming muddy. After several days of rain, it does soften up somewhat, but it never becomes a muddy soup, and once the weather clears, it quickly drains and returns to its former state. In winter, it's durable enough that we can drive the tractor over it to plow it and keep a small area clear. It's easy to pick manure off it as well—the manure doesn't freeze to the ground as it does with more organic soil. Adding this footing material was one of the best horsekeeping decisions we've made.

4. The Realities of Horse Ownership

HORSE OWNERSHIP IS not all sunshine and butterflies. Certainly, there are days when the sunshine and butterflies abound, and we live for those days! However, there are some challenges to maintaining your farmette, which I will discuss here.

Finding Time to Ride

You may imagine that once your horses live at your house, you will have all the time in the world to ride. What could be easier? They're literally *in* your backyard! Sadly, the reality is not always so simple. Once you finish all the stall cleaning, water bucket scrubbing, raking, sweeping, fence repairs, blanket changes, and fly spraying, there may not be much time left in the day for actual riding. And those are just the daily chores—I haven't even mentioned all the occasional but time-consuming tasks, like putting in a new fence line, turning the manure pile or spreading manure, mowing the fields, building stalls or shelters, putting in new footing in your sacrifice paddocks, and so on. I'm not gonna lie—horses are extremely time-consuming.

The key to having enough time to ride is to make it a priority for yourself. I work at home and would seem to have the leisure to ride whenever I want to. But many a day has gone by when I don't get to ride because other things seem more important—meeting that work deadline, doing laundry, making dinner, working in the garden. Having a young child complicates matters as well, since I can't just go off on a trail ride and leave my toddler at home alone (see below for more on that topic). The solution, I have found, is to make riding my first priority, and to schedule it into my week. I have a scheduled lesson at 10:30 each Monday, so I know my trainer will arrive at that time, and I *will* ride. It's not optional. Each week I look at my schedule, in terms of work and available childcare, and choose times when I plan to ride. Then I stick to my plan. No, I don't ride every day, but I do ride three or four times a week, which is much better than I was doing before I started planning my ride times.

Another way to stay motivated is to set clear goals for yourself. This is one of the main reasons I show. If I have a dressage show coming up on June 25, I know I'd better be riding at least three times a week until then, or the show is not going to go well. If you don't enjoy showing, try to find other goals for yourself. These can be training goals—"I will teach Ginger to cross water by the end of the month"—or numerical goals—"I will ride four times a week every week in June"—or event-specific goals—"I will properly condition my horse for a ten-mile group trail ride scheduled for October 24."

You also need to get used to imperfect circumstances. Coming from a riding stable, you may be accustomed to being provided with ideal conditions for riding. There's an arena with well-maintained footing, and if it rains, snows, or gets dark before you make it to the barn, there's an indoor with lights. There are readily available com-

BELOW: Scheduled weekly lessons with my trainer, shown here riding Beamer, keep me honest and motivated about my riding goals.

panions for trail rides, and taking a lesson or getting some training is as easy as scheduling it in. At home, you may not have an arena at all. You may have to ride on grass, which gets slippery and muddy when it rains. You may have to ride on the side of the road. If you need an arena to practice your specific discipline, you may have to load up and trailer to an arena, where you may have to pay a fee to use it. You may have to trail ride alone, with rocks and roots underfoot and tree branches hitting you in the face, since you haven't had time to trim them yet this year. In short, you have to deal with it.

When we first moved to our little farm, I believed I had "nowhere to ride." I tried riding in the field, but it was too hilly for my taste. If it rained or snowed, I simply didn't ride at all. I found that I was hardly riding my horses at all. As time went on, I adapted to my circumstances. I've discovered that I have lots of places to ride! My hilly field—well, as long as it's not muddy, the hills are great for conditioning and learning to balance at various gaits and through transitions. When it is muddy, I can ride along the road. There's a long dirt road not far from my house, and it's great for riding. My neighbor's trails are right across the street—all it took was a friendly request, and I can ride on them. Miracle of miracles, another horsey neighbor about a fifteen-minute trail ride away decided to put in a small arena, and she's happy to share it with me.

I also believed for a long time that I couldn't ride unless someone else was available to ride with me, since my horse was "too herd-bound." This is a common problem for horses accustomed to the stable environment, where other horses are always around. The solution was to put on my big girl panties and do some training (see page 227 for tips). My horse is now a willing partner, happy to head down the trail on his own because it means a new adventure for him.

Horses and Children

Having horses and young children at the same time can be quite a challenge. The best steps you can take to ensure your continued sanity are to adjust your expectations and to have a strong support network.

For new parents, horses may need to take a backseat. The baby will be the most important responsibility that you have. You and your partner must have an open and harmonious relationship, in which each steps up to take on tasks as needed. While the baby is your number one priority, the horses still need basic care regardless. Someone will have to go out to feed, water, and clean stalls or sheds, at a bare minimum. In very cold, hot, or rainy weather, you probably won't want to take your newborn outside with you to do chores, so

BELOW: Introduce your children to the horses from day one to minimize their fears.

make sure you have a backup plan. Consider hiring help for at least the first few weeks, so you can focus on your baby.

Once the baby is old enough, you can bring her out with you. Being outdoors around animals is *good* for children. But do make sure you take appropriate safety precautions. Park the stroller or play pen in a place where horses can't get to it. It may be tempting to carry an infant in a carrier while you go about your chores, but be sure never to handle your horses while carrying the child. Things can go wrong very quickly.

Make sure older children know the safety rules, and never leave a child alone with a horse. When you can, try to involve your kids in the horse chores rather than expecting them to play independently while you work. Even a very young child can wield a miniature pitchfork to help clean stalls, carry a flake of hay to a paddock, and help dump pre-measured grain into buckets. They can help brush a quiet horse, and you can engage them in conversation, teaching them about all the parts of the horse and equipment as you tack up.

A newborn baby is far more time-consuming than new parents can possibly imagine. As far as riding goes, it may be best to take a planned vacation from the saddle after the birth of a child. For the mother, her body needs time to heal, and if she's breastfeeding, she won't want to be too far from her infant for long. These are important bonding days, so don't stress too much about saddle time. The horses will still be there when you're ready.

LEFT Once your kids are old enough to ride with you, you've got it made!

When that time comes, child care will be your main hurdle to overcome. Partners can trade off time caring for the child and time spent with the horses. But if one or both parents are working away from the farm, time is at a premium. This is where your strong support network comes in. There are several ways to score an hour or two to work your horse: A grandparent may be thrilled to come over and spend some time with the little one. Befriend other local moms with children the same age as your own, and schedule play dates that can double as child care opportunities—she'll come over and watch the kids while you ride one day, and the next you can go to her house and watch the kids while she gardens, for example. Another option is to hire a mother's helper. This is a young person similar to a babysitter who comes to your home to help you out with the children. Since you are still home and physically present, a mother's helper can be quite a bit younger, and therefore less expensive, than a true babysitter, who would be expected to care for children in the parents' absence. If you're lucky, you might find a horse-crazy teen who is willing to trade child-care time for riding time.

My own daughter is now three years old, and she goes to preschool three days a week. While she's gone, I try to maximize my work time so I can call it a day at about 3 PM. This leaves me an hour and a half to tack up, ride, untack, clean up, and turn the horse back out before I go pick up my daughter. It's a tight schedule, but I manage. I don't have much choice!

Aside from all the scheduling concerns, having children and horses together can bring added joy to your household. My daughter is learning to ride, bringing a sense of fulfillment and completeness to my life. I look forward eagerly to the day when she has her own pony, and we can go for family trail rides. Even now, she loves to help Mama with the chores, picking stalls and dumping grain with enthusiasm. She is learning at a very early age to have compassion and care for other living beings and for nature. These are lessons I hope she will carry throughout her life, whether or not she turns out to be a horse-crazy person.

Brown Mill Farm

Sandy and Terry Swett have raised eight children in their rambling farmhouse, and currently keep four horses in the attached antique barn at their Brown Mill Farm. Willie is a twenty-two-year-old Lippitt Morgan gelding who belongs to the Swetts' daughter, Erin, a nursing student. Nortena is a fourteen-year-old Paso Fino; Faby is a fifteen-year-old Cheval Canadien; and their newest addition, Maimie, is a fourteen-year-old Clydesdale mare. The Swett women are primarily trail riders, although Erin has studied and shown dressage as well. She notes, "I've trained in dressage, Western, jumping, side saddle, saddleseat. Everything." The family also loves to drive, and son-in-law Jeff breeds and shows Belgian driving horses. Willie came to the family as an experienced driving horse, so Sandy and Erin bought a cart and Jeff taught them to drive.

The farm has a small arena, which Erin used to use regularly when she was showing, but now it sits mainly unused. They have a four-horse gooseneck trailer, which Sandy says she uses "all the time. We go camping sometimes, so we'll trailer the horses and go camping. There's a mattress over the gooseneck. We can trailer them to the vet instead of having the vet come here."

The horses come into their stalls at night, except in the hot summer, when they go out at night and stay in during the daytime. "There's always a breeze blowing through that barn," Sandy notes with satisfaction. She describes the daily routine at Brown Mill Farm. "We put them in at night because we like to handle them, and make sure they have manners. We shovel stalls every morning, and really it doesn't take very long. We get a load of sawdust delivered, and it doesn't take much work. They have fresh water every day, and we have hot and cold running water in the barn. In the wintertime we don't have to go outside at all. We go from the house through the carriage house to the barn. We have a scuttle in the barn, and we keep a wheelbarrow down in the basement." These old-fashioned conveniences are a blessing even on a modern horse farm.

Although she grew up around horses, Erin didn't learn to ride until age ten. "I was afraid of them. I hated them," she recalls. "Then my sister forced me to ride when I was ten, and I liked it. When I was fourteen I went and stayed with a trainer in New Jersey for six weeks of hard-core training, and learned all different kinds of riding. He took me to Kentucky and we bought Willie, and I came back here and kept training and did dressage shows. My sister and I showed driving horses when I was seventeen."

Sandy knew she loved horses from a very young age. "I wanted to ride when I was young, but my parents wouldn't let me. I drove the pony next door, Pepper, and he was a nasty little thing. He bucked and he kicked, and he'd take me over stone walls, flip the cart—but I never gave up my love for horses. When I got married that was the first thing I did—I went and bought my first pony, a good-sized Welsh pony named Chubby, and it was like the blind leading the blind. Then I bought a buckskin Quarter Horse, Toby, and he was just awesome—a great, great, great horse. And I've been in horses ever since.

I love horses. That's *my* time. I go out in the barn and just work with them."

I asked Erin what it was like to grow up in a family with so many children and also have horses at the same time. How did Sandy manage it all? "We always had older sisters, so she always had babysitters. We always had very safe horses, so we could take the kids riding at a very young age. When we were real little, we were just always outside, out in the barn, so we were used to it."

Sandy concedes that in some ways, boarding her horses might be easier. "If they're at a facility, you can just show up and work with them. Whereas when they're at home, it's like, oh, I have to water my garden or this or that." However, she says she would never consider boarding, because the advantages of keeping horses at home far outweigh any benefit of keeping them at a stable. "I never come in the door at night without hollering to them, and they whinny to me," Sandy says with a smile. "They look for me to do that. I mess with my horses a lot, I interact with them a lot, which I don't think a lot of people do. You talk about living the dream—this is my dream right here, a farmhouse with horses. And a barn. I love having my barn. I keep my barn cleaner than my house." She describes one of the greatest joys of having horses: "I like to hear crunching. I like to go in a clean barn, and hear crunch, crunch, crunch. That's satisfaction. Clean horses, clean bedding, clean barn, and crunching. That's music to my ears."

Can I Ever Go On Vacation Again?

Yes, you can! You will have to hire help to watch over your farm and do chores while you're gone. There are a few things you can do to make it as easy as possible for you to leave your farm for a long weekend.

1. Establish a working relationship with a professional, responsible, horse-savvy caregiver well in advance of your planned trip. Have her come out at least once to meet the horses and learn your system. Treat her well and pay her well, since a caregiver who knows your horses is invaluable. Have a backup person prepared in case an emergency befalls your primary sitter.

2. Practice 24/7 turnout. If your horses live outdoors all the time, it is vastly easier for their caregiver. The person who comes in to feed won't have to handle the horses much (as she would have to do when turning out or bringing in stall-kept horses). And mucking-out tasks will be minimized as well.

3. Have the horses out on pasture, or if pasture is not available or insufficient, feed round bales. If the horses have access to grass or hay at all times, there is less risk of them going hungry if

your caregiver does not show up, as well as less risk of boredom-related accidents or escape attempts.

4. By the same token, provide a backup water source. If you normally water with one seventy-gallon trough, add a second one before you leave. That way if one goes dry or the horses dump it (as mine tend to do when they get bored) they will have another option.

5. Be sure your fences are as secure as possible. Check that all electric fences are functioning properly and that all parts of the fences and gates are in good repair. If possible, your farm should have a perimeter fence that fully encloses it, so that even if a horse does escape from a paddock or stall, he's still confined to your property.

6. Prominently post a sign listing contact information for you, your caregiver, your vet, and any other people who might be able to help in an emergency situation. Also post detailed instructions on the feeding and care of the animals, both as a reminder to your caregiver and as a backup plan in case someone else needs to come in and help out if, say, the planned caregiver has an emergency and can't come.

BELOW: Providing round bales means the horses should never be out of hay.

7. Inform your neighbors that you'll be away, and ask that they call you if anything seems amiss at your property.

It does take some extra planning and forethought, and there is the added expense of hiring a horse-sitter, but there is no reason you can't schedule a vacation or weekend away. The most important points are to find a sitter that you trust and to make your system as simple and foolproof as possible.

Disaster Preparedness

We don't like to think about it, but there are some worst-case-scenario situations that can affect your horses and farm. What if you become seriously ill or injured? What if there's a flood or a barn fire? What if you have to evacuate due to wildfires or a hurricane? What if you get into a car accident and don't make it home from work? What if—heaven forbid—you were to die? What would happen to your horses in these situations?

Much like vacation planning, disaster planning involves setting up your whole system in a way that it would be easy for someone else to step in and take over your role as caregiver. Overly complex feeding and turnout requirements should be streamlined. Review the list for vacation planning above, and make sure your system fits the bill. Keep two or three people in mind who know your horses and your system, whom you could call in the event of a personal emergency.

If you have to evacuate and can't bring your animals, there's not much that can be done. However, they will be *far* better off if you leave them turned out with shelter, round bales or pasture, and plenty of water, than confined in stalls where they will quickly run out of food and water. If your horses are accustomed to living outdoors, they will be unfazed by the change. They may miss a few grain meals, but hopefully you'll be able to return home in a few days and they'll be none the worse for the wear.

How Many Horses Can I Have?

You choose to keep horses at home because you love horses. A lot. That's a given. That's what makes it so easy to shout, "YES!" when someone offers you a free horse. Look at his adorable soft nose and his cute fuzzy ears—how can you say no? Besides, he'll be perfect for your daughter in a few years, right?

It's a fact of life in these tough economic times that free or cheap horses are extremely easy to come by. Once your local horse community discovers that you provide a safe home with excellent care, you will find yourself overwhelmed by the offers of free horses from owners who are only too eager to find a good home for their beloved but no-longer-needed pets. You may also fall victim to the allure of the Internet, where auction sites, rescue organizations, and Craigslist tempt you with photos of underfed, rain-rot-ridden, neglected creatures just crying out for your love and TLC. Or maybe you hear about a friend-of-a-friend whose divorce is forcing the fire-sale of her show horse at a bargain price.

Occasionally, these opportunities can work out well for you, and you can gain a nice riding horse at little or no up-front cost. However, just because the horse is free to acquire doesn't mean it's free to keep! Horseman's wisdom states that there's "no such thing as a free horse." Before taking on any new horse, carefully assess your budget's ability to absorb the additional costs of hay, grain, shavings, farrier, and vet bills. Will you have to build another stall? Buy new blankets, tack, buckets, and grooming supplies? Can your pastures handle the added burden of another hungry mouth and destructive hooves? If the horse is coming from an auction or a questionable home, are you equipped to quarantine the new horse for two weeks or more? (For more on quarantine requirements, see page 139.) How about time . . . do you really have the time to give another horse the love, attention, and training that he will require?

I know that right now, my personal maximum for time and money is three horses. My facilities can handle up to six horses if some of those are boarders. It would be easy for me to acquire multiple free horses right now. All I'd have to do would be to make a few phone calls to friends who I know are looking to place their horses in good homes, and I could have five trailers pulling up to deliver them to me tomorrow. A dream come true, right? Wrong. The result would be that each of them would receive inadequate care, since I don't have time in my day to pay individual attention to each of them. I also know that the quality and quantity of their feed might be forced to diminish, since I simply could not afford to offer them each as much top-quality hay as they need. Their annual vet bills would likely have to go on credit—*never* a good financial plan. Finally, my pastures would be stressed beyond their capabilities, and all my lovely grass would be destroyed within weeks.

It's best to set a limit for yourself ahead of time, and be strict with yourself when it comes to each new equine acquisition. I'm not saying that it's never okay to take in a horse in need. I am saying that you need to pay careful attention to your bottom line, both in terms of cost and time, when considering whether it makes sense for *you*.

Am I Better Off Boarding?

For many people, boarding is the better option for horse ownership. Keeping horses at home is not just a hobby—it's a lifestyle. Are you willing to accept its challenges? Do you truly enjoy the dirty work of caring for horses—cleaning stalls, putting up hay, mowing pastures, mending fences—and, indeed, do you have time for all these tasks? Or would you rather just show up and ride? Only you can answer these questions. If your priorities are to have easy access to training and instruction, plenty of time to ride, a well-maintained arena and indoor, and a barn community, then it may be the case that boarding is the better option for you, and there's no shame in making that choice. If your priorities are to share a life with your horses, to have full control over their daily care, to get to know them as well on the ground as you do from the saddle, and to live the farm lifestyle, then keeping horses at home is the right choice for you.

Can I Make Money from My Horse Farm?

Keep in the forefront of your mind the old joke, "How do you make a small fortune in the horse business? Start with a large fortune." Making money with horses is notoriously difficult. They're expensive, risky, and can die or become unrideable for a wide variety of unexpected reasons. In fact, I've heard many people say their financial advisers suggested that they get into horse breeding or sales *in order to show a loss on their business* and reduce their taxes owed.

One of the limiting factors in starting a horse business on your property may be insurance. Before you do anything else, call your insurance agent and get a quote for adding a liability rider covering boarding other peoples' horses on your property, as well as any liability coverage needed for riding other peoples' horses for money (training), teaching riding, or having people ride on your property. The cost for these types of insurance can be high—even prohibitively high if you're planning to run a small-scale operation. It pays to shop around and to choose a company or representative that's knowledgeable about the specific types of insurance required for a horse business.

Common wisdom among savvy horse people states that no one makes money by boarding. Most commercial stables actually make their money by other means, such as lessons, training, and horse sales, all of which are beyond the scope of the novice horse owner. The costs of maintaining a farm and caring for horses are so high that, at best, you can hope to break even. If you calculate merely the direct costs of horse care—feed and bedding—it may appear that you can make some money. But if you include the costs of maintaining your farm, extra insurance needed, and your own labor as a monetary figure, you'll see that it doesn't add up to much, if any, profit.

On the other hand, your goal may not be to make a large profit. Your reason for having a boarder may be to provide a buddy to trail ride with, or a companion for your solo horse at no cost to yourself. In my case, we have one boarder who helps offset the cost of hay for my other three. Since we're maintaining the farm for our own horses anyway, there's not much additional cost involved in having the one boarder. Labor, similarly, is not much greater than it would be for our three—we'd still have to muck out the shed, scrub the water trough, and put up hay almost as often for three horses as for four. So having our one boarder does provide a little money in our pockets to buy feed for all four. We certainly are not making any profit, but there is still value to us in having her here.

Another way to add to the bottom line is to provide a value-added service for which you can charge a premium rate. A good example is retirement board. If you have large pastures with roomy run-in sheds, you may be in an ideal position to offer retirement board for absentee owners. In such a case, the horse's owner, who may live at a distance or even out of state, pays extra for you to perform *all* aspects of the horse's daily care, from grooming and hoof-picking to blanket changes and fly spraying to deworming and scheduling vet and far-rier services. This works especially well for a farm located in an area where land is not as expensive to acquire. A hundred-acre retirement farm in upstate New York might cater to retired show horses whose wealthy owners live in Connecticut or Westchester County. Or a farm in rural West Virginia might draw clients from affluent horsey areas in Virginia and the Carolinas. The keys to success are to know how to save money without compromising the quality of horse care (such as buying supplies in bulk); doing the majority of the work yourself rather than hiring it out; offering quality services so that you can charge a premium and clients will still feel they're getting a good deal; and knowing your limits.

At the other end of the spectrum is pasture board or rough board. This might be a profitable option for someone who has a large farm with plenty of pasture and stalls, but not very much time to devote to horse care. In such a setup, you rent pasture or stall space to horse owners for a relatively low dollar amount, and they are expected to provide all feed, bedding, and daily care for their own horses, including feeding, turnout, and stall cleaning. This can work well, but has its own inherent set of risks, such as owners who fail to provide adequate care for their horses on your property.

Generating Income

When you have a lot of farm property and the time to invest in its development, there are a multitude of ways to generate additional income, some horse-related and some not. Many of these ideas are dependent on your own areas of expertise and interest, as well as your available land and facilities. These lists should serve as inspiration and starting points for generating your own ideas. Of course, you'll need to consider the requisite insurance, tax, zoning, and permit issues for each.

Horse-Related Income

- Carriage rides or hayrides, either on your property, at events such as weddings and county fairs, or around town on special occasions
- Haunted hayrides at Halloween
- Pony rides and pony parties
- Summer camp (for kids or adults)
- Trail riding for the public
- Horse-focused bed-and-breakfast that allows people to board their horses while staying in your guest cottage or in-law apartment for a trail-riding vacation
- Hosting horse shows, clinics with celebrity trainers, and hunter-paces or group trail rides

General Farm Income

- Organic produce (for a small-scale farmer it can be beneficial to focus on one or two specific "niche" crops rather than a wide variety)
- Cut flowers
- Pick-your-own apples, strawberries, pumpkins, or other seasonal fruits
- Raising and selling livestock such as goats, sheep, poultry, or cows
- Raising chickens for organic, farm-raised eggs or meat
- Short-term boarding of dogs or cats
- Christmas tree farm
- Producing and selling firewood
- Making and selling hay
- Making and selling maple syrup and maple sugar products
- Renting out indoor arena time to other interests, such as dog trainers or dog agility groups

Part ②

Finding a
Horse

5. Riding Styles

ONCE YOUR HORSE property is ready and you're confident in your knowledge of horse care, it's time for the fun part—start looking for a horse! You should have already learned a lot about daily care and veterinary matters from your trainer while taking lessons, but if you need a refresher, turn to Part 3 of this book and read up. Meanwhile, start browsing classified ads and networking through your local equestrian contacts as you develop a mental image of your ideal horse. The first thing to consider is your choice of discipline. This has a great effect on what type of horse you will be looking for.

Virtually all horses kept at home should be able to double as trail horses, even if their primary sport is dressage, reining, or another competitive discipline. There will be many days when you don't want to head into the arena for schooling, and the trails are calling your name. You also want to have a horse that's safe and sane enough to take on fun excursions like hunter-paces or overnight camping vacations. Not every horse is cut out to be a trail horse, so when you're horse-shopping, make sure this is a priority on your list. If you plan to do any trail riding at all, that hot-house flower of a show hunter may prove to be frustrating when you try to head out for a quiet hack and he comes unglued because he's never seen so many trees in one place before.

Many (not all) horses can be trained to accept, and even love, trail riding, but the process can be lengthy and requires patience and skill if the horse is hot, spooky, or terrified. Life will be far easier for you if you seek out horses that are experienced on the trails. Ideally, find one that will hack out alone as well as in company. You won't always have a companion to ride with, and a horse that's happy enough to head down the trail alone is a godsend.

If your primary goal is trail riding, and you don't plan to show or ride in any kind of arena-based discipline, you can narrow your search still further. Although many people choose a Quarter Horse or other stock type for trail riding, breed is less relevant than temperament and training. Look for a horse that's calm and steady, as close to bombproof as possible, surefooted, and experienced on the trails. The ideal candidate is on the shorter side of 16 hands (for easier mounting without a mounting block in the wilderness) yet sturdy enough to carry weight over long periods of time, and with the endurance to stay fit and fresh. Look for hard, solid hooves that will hold up against

RIGHT: Robin's size and temperament make her an ideal trail horse.

rocky terrain, and stocky conformation with legs that are predisposed to soundness. Sloping pastern and shoulder angles indicate an easy-to-ride trot.

An added bonus is a temperament that allows the horse to behave the same whether he's being worked regularly or hasn't done a thing in three months. I have had both types. Beamer is a great horse and a rock star on the trails if he's being ridden four or five days a week, but my life often (almost always) prevents me from riding that much. If he's had a few days off in a row, he's hot and fresh and very difficult to ride. Robin, on the other hand, is the same calm and willing partner whether I last rode her yesterday or six months ago. In trying to balance riding with children, work, and a social life, I've learned to really appreciate that quality.

Competitive Trail and Endurance

Competitive trail and endurance take trail riding to the next level. Arabians are by far the most common breed seen in endurance, since they have been bred for stamina, endurance, and speed over distance. Competitive trail horses can be any breed, but Quarter Horses, Arabians, Arab crosses, and Morgans are common. *North American Trail Ride Conference: www.natrc.org. American Endurance Ride Conference: www.aerc.org. FEI: www.fei.org/disciplines/endurance.*

Western Disciplines

Western styles of riding all evolved from the horsemanship of the cowboys of the American West. Tack, rider apparel, and riding styles are all based in traditions of utility on the cattle ranches of the West. Cowboys needed to ride with one hand while swinging a lariat, so they developed neck reining. They needed a place to dally a rope after lassoing a calf, so the saddle horn emerged. They needed protection from the sun and rain while riding the range, so the wide-brimmed cowboy hat became the headgear of choice for Western riders, even in the show ring of today. They needed to be able to ride all day long on a comfortable horse, so American Quarter Horses were bred for a smooth, steady, easy-to-sit trot.

Most horses used for Western riding are Quarter Horses or another stock-type breed such as Paint or Appaloosa. Even within these breeds, however, there are a variety of types, so look for a horse bred and trained for your specific discipline. There are "halter" type horses that are generally unsuitable for riding. Horses bred and trained for the show ring may excel in Western pleasure, with slow, easy-to-ride gaits, long legs, and an elegant head carriage. Performance horses intended for speed or cattle events tend to be stocky and agile, with catlike reflexes and bursts of speed ideal for barrel racing, reining, team penning, or cutting. Quarter Horses are generally known for their calm temperaments and trainability, making them excellent candidates for novice horse owners. (As with any breed stereotype, however, you should keep it in mind, but consider the individual horse. I have met some nutty Quarter Horses in my day!)

Western Pleasure and Western Equitation

Western pleasure and Western equitation (also called Western riding) are known as "rail classes," meaning that the horses show in a group along the rail at a walk, jog, and lope. Pleasure classes judge the horse, while equitation classes judge the rider. Judges look for a relaxed walk and a flat-kneed, slow-legged jog and lope. The rider's cues should be so subtle as to be nearly imperceptible to the casual observer.

The ideal Western pleasure horse has long legs, a slender neck, and a delicate head, and is trained to the hilt. For the top levels of competition, look for a horse of your chosen breed (usually Quarter Horse, but also Paint, Appaloosa, Arabian, or a number of other breeds) that has been specifically bred, trained, and marketed for

ABOVE: Western pleasure horse.

the Western pleasure arena, and expect to pay top dollar for a top prospect. For local showing or pleasure riding, look for a nice stock-type breed, trained Western, with a mellow, easygoing temperament. *United States Equestrian Federation: www.usef.org. American Quarter Horse Association: www.aqha.com.*

Cattle Events: Cutting, Team Penning, Working Cow Horse

Quarter Horses seem to have a natural affinity for cows and for controlling and working with cows. Various Western events revolve around working cattle. Cutting is perhaps the most spectacular of these events. A horse and rider enter a pen containing several cattle, choose one cow to cut from the herd, and separate it from its companions. Then the rider drops the reins and allows the horse to work independently to keep the cow from returning to the herd. A cutting horse must know and understand its job, must be naturally "cowy"— that is, have a good instinct for working cattle—and be quick and agile. *National Cutting Horse Association: www.nchacutting.com.*

Team penning is a team sport that requires three horses and riders to cut three specific cattle from a large herd and guide them into a separate holding pen, while preventing the rest of the herd from entering the pen. This is a timed event—the riders have 60 to 90 seconds to complete the task. This can be a great sport for a family to learn together, so each member of the family can be part of the same team. Much like cutting horses, horses used in team penning must be cowy, fast, and agile. *United States Team Penning Association: www. ustpa.com.*

Barrel Racing

Barrel racing is a speed event in which horse and rider gallop through a cloverleaf pattern with a barrel in each "leaf." Each horse and rider pair competes individually, and the pair with the fastest time wins. Missing a barrel results in disqualification, and knocking over a barrel results in a five-second time penalty. Barrel racing was originally developed as a rodeo event for women, as opposed to roping and bronc riding, which were the domain of men. Barrel horses must be fast and agile, able to accelerate quickly and make extremely tight and accurate turns at high speed. *National Barrel Horse Association: www.nbha.com.*

ABOVE: Many Quarter Horses have a natural instinct for seeking out and chasing cows.

Reining

Reining is the only Western discipline recognized by the FEI—the international governing body for equestrian sports. It has been an Olympic competition since 2006. Reining requires the horse and rider to complete a designated series of movements at the lope and gallop, including flying lead changes, circles, spins, rollbacks, reinbacks, and the spectacular sliding stop. Judging is based on control and obedience, finesse, attitude, quickness, and authority. Reining

horses must be athletic, balanced, obedient, agile, and adjustable. *National Reining Horse Association: http://nrha1.com. FEI: www.fei.org/ disciplines/reining.*

English Disciplines

The English disciplines include dressage, eventing, and hunter/ jumpers. In general, I have observed that hunter/jumper riders tend to be more likely to keep their horses at stables, where they have easy access to training, jumps, and shows, than eventers, who tend to be more self-reliant and gritty, or dressage riders, who don't need as much access to specialized facilities. These are certainly generalizations, and of course there are many hunters kept at home or dressage horses kept at stables.

Dressage

"Dressage" is literally the French word for "training." It is the foundation of all the English disciplines, although it does not involve jumping. At the lower levels, it involves training the horse to accept the bridle, to lift his back and softly accept the rider's weight, to move freely forward at all gaits, and to bend and flex in response to the rider's aids. The upper levels introduce higher concepts such as self-carriage, extended and collected gaits, lateral work including half-pass and shoulder-in, and specialized movements such as piaffe, passage, and flying lead changes.

Any horse on the planet, as long as it is sound, is capable of performing lower-level dressage work. Dressage, as they say, is good for every horse. If you simply want to learn the fundamentals of lower level dressage, or dabble in some arena work to complement your trail riding, almost any horse of any breed can be suitable. Look for a partner who has a good start in the basics, such as working on the bit and moving steadily and confidently forward and straight in all gaits, to have the greatest enjoyment and success as you begin your dressage journey.

Riders who wish to be competitive in the dressage arena and move steadily up the levels need to invest considerable time in searching for the right mount. The right horse will have a good mind—that is, willing, intelligent, trainable, and eager to please. He will have excellent conformation for dressage, allowing him to lengthen his stride for the extended gaits or sit and elevate his stride for collected work. He will have three good gaits—a pure, four-beat, flowing walk; a forward, open, lofty trot; and a consistent, balanced, three-beat canter. Many competitive dressage riders seek out warmbloods for dressage, which makes sense, as these horses have been bred for generations to have top-notch gaits and athleticism for this type of work (see page 118 for more on warmbloods). In addition, some classical dressage riders prefer so-called Baroque breeds, such as Friesians, Andalusians, and Lusitanos, whose conformation lends itself easily to self-carriage and collection. However, breed is less important than good conformation, gaits, and mind. Unless you're shooting for

ABOVE: A dressage horse and rider seem to function as one mind and body.

the Olympics, don't rule out a nice, sporty Arabian, Thoroughbred, or even a draft cross just because he's the "wrong" breed, if his inherent qualities suit your needs. *United States Dressage Federation: www.usdf. org. FEI: www.fei.org/disciplines/dressage.*

Eventing

Eventing is a discipline that combines three distinct phases—dressage, cross-country, and stadium jumping. Dressage demonstrates that the horse is well trained, obedient, and supple. The cross-country phase consists of a lengthy gallop through open fields and over solid natural jumps, demonstrating the horse's boldness, athleticism, and endurance. Finally, the stadium jumping phase (also called show jumping) returns the horse to the show ring for a course of fences, demonstrating his stamina (since he is still recovering from the rigors of cross-country) as well as his willingness and athleticism over fences. Many people consider eventing to be the ultimate test of a horse-and-rider pair.

Despite its physical challenges, eventing has never been a sport of breed snobbery. Since it places less emphasis on quality of movement than dressage or hunters, one needn't buy a fancy imported warmblood in order to be competitive. At the lower levels, any horse with the conformation and trainability for jumping can be appropriate. At the upper levels, the horses with the innate endurance and athleticism to endure the cross-country phase and jump the big jumps have historically been Thoroughbreds. Thus, a rider with a good eye for conformation and potential can pick up her next great eventing partner as a bargain-basement racetrack reject. At the top of the sport these days, however, warmbloods are making inroads against the Thoroughbreds. This is largely due to the change from the classical "long format" for three-day events to the new "short format," which places less emphasis on endurance and correspondingly more emphasis on dressage and jumping ability.

As an eventing newbie, however, the single most important quality to look for in a prospect (after soundness, of course) is experience in eventing. Be sure the horses you consider have proven themselves

RIGHT: Eventer competing in the cross-country phase.

on the cross-country course. Galloping and jumping at speed over solid obstacles can be an unnerving prospect for both horse and rider, so it's best if at least one of the two has been there, done that. Once you as a rider have gained some experience and moved up the levels with your veteran mount, you can think about taking on a prospect to bring along with the help of a good trainer. In any horse sport it's best to start with a knowledgeable horse, but this is especially true in eventing, where cross-country can be very dangerous for an unskilled pair. *United States Eventing Association: http://useventing.com. FEI: www.fei.org/disciplines/eventing.*

Hunter/Jumper

There are actually several sub-disciplines under the heading of "hunter/jumper." The uniting factor is that they all involve show jumping, and usually compete at the same shows. The three main types of hunter/jumper competition are hunters, jumpers, and equitation. In the hunter divisions, the horse is judged on its style, way of going, and manners as it completes a course of jumps. There are also flat classes (with no jumps), sometimes called "under saddle classes," within each hunter division in which multiple horses compete together at a walk, trot, and canter and are judged subjectively for movement and manners at all gaits. Hunter divisions are divided into professional and amateur categories, as well as by maximum height of the jumps, age of the rider, greenness of the horse, or emphasis (such as conformation hunter classes in which the horse's conformation is heavily weighted).

In the jumpers, judging is objective and is based purely on speed and accuracy (that is, not knocking down any rails), with no emphasis on style or gaits. Courses tend to be much more technical than in the hunter divisions. The highest level of jumper competition is Grand Prix, with fence heights of up to 5'3" and spreads of up to 6 feet. There are no flat classes in the jumper divisions.

In the equitation division (also called hunt seat equitation), the rider's position and effectiveness are judged, both over fences and in a flat class. Although the horse is not specifically being judged, a well-trained horse is obviously a great asset to the rider, allowing her to show off her abilities as well as possible. In the more advanced equitation classes, courses can be quite technical, requiring the horse and rider to execute such movements as counter-canter, rollbacks, and flying changes. In certain classes, the judge may require the horse and rider to complete various "tests," such as halt, rein-back, hand gallop, figure-eight, or riding without stirrups.

When shopping for a hunter/jumper, it's important to know which division you plan to compete in. Although any hunter or jumper must have good conformation and training for jumping, the styles vary so greatly that most horses tend to specialize in one of the three divisions, based largely on their individual temperaments and talents. A hunter must be tractable and calm, responsive to the rider's subtle aids, and scopey and stylish over fences. He also must have the long-strided, flat-kneed movement desired in the hunter ring. A jumper should be bold, fast, athletic, and agile. An equitation horse should be something of a mix of the two, with a hunter's temperament and trainability but the agility and power of a jumper.

Not surprisingly, at the higher levels of hunter/jumper competition we find mainly warmbloods. These sport horses have been purpose-bred for generations, with certain bloodlines specializing in hunters or jumpers. For a rider planning to compete at the regional or national level, a warmblood sport horse is a virtual necessity. However, so is a stable with full training and care, and a virtually unlimited budget. For the most part, riders who keep their horses at home will be competing at a somewhat lower level. For local or even state-level showing, a variety of breeds can excel. Perhaps the most common non-warmblood breed in the hunter/jumper ring is the Thoroughbred, followed by Quarter Horses. Ponies, of course, are huge in the hunter world for young children.

For any breed, the priorities when shopping for a hunter or jumper are conformation, athleticism, jumping ability, and temperament, with the additions of style over fences and movement for hunters, or speed and scope for jumpers. A well-trained, high-quality hunter, jumper, or equitation mount capable of trotting into the show ring tomorrow is going to cost you a pretty penny. Perhaps more than any other discipline, the hunter/jumper world is an expensive one. If you have the experience and ability to train the horse yourself, you can save a little by buying a young prospect to bring along. Or you can limit your competition goals to the local or state level, and plan to have a lot of fun with a safe, pleasant horse that didn't cost five figures or more. *United States Hunter/Jumper Association: www.ushja.org. FEI: www.fei.org/disciplines/jumping.*

BELOW: Competitor in the jumper division.

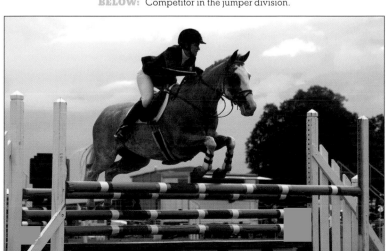

Foxhunting

by Steven D. Price

The image of foxhunting, of scarlet-coated riders astride long-limbed Thoroughbreds galloping across fields and over fences behind hounds in pursuit of a fox, is only partially correct. You can hunt on virtually any breed or type of horse, not jump or even gallop if you wish, and during the early part of the hunting season you can wear just about any kind of riding apparel you wish.

In addition to two or more hours of cross-country riding in the company of like-minded equestrians, foxhunting gives you the opportunity to watch a pack of well-trained foxhounds search out and, if they find, chase after a fox (some hunts pursue coyotes, while others hunt both). A run may go on for a short distance or for many miles, and almost all will end when the quarry "goes to ground," the term for ducking into a hole or culvert or any other refuge. True, foxes and coyotes are occasionally caught and killed, but if your feelings toward blood sports cause you to shudder, just ask farmers how they feel about losing poultry to four-legged predators and you'll learn why landowners welcome hunting across their land.

The season is divided into two parts. "Cubbing," when young hounds are entered into the pack, starts in late summer. It's a time when all riders wear informal "ratcatcher" clothing; some hunts don't object to polo shirts and chaps over jeans. The formal season begins in October or November, depending on the part of country. That's when gentlemen members wear their scarlet coats, women wear black, and everyone wears a stock tie or choker. A "field" (which is how the followers are collectively referred to) in such attire is a lovely sight, and such tradition is also part of the sport's appeal.

Many novices begin by "hilltopping," which is following at the rear of the field and at a sedate pace. Jumping is either optional or not at all.

ABOVE: Author Steven D. Price riding Guitar while out cubbing with Virginia's Blue Ridge Hunt.

More than 170 hunts in the United States and Canada are registered with the Masters of Foxhounds Association. In addition, there are many informal private and "farmer" packs all over the country. *For further information: Masters of Foxhounds Association, www.mfha.org and its* Covertside *magazine, www.ecovertside. net. See also Fox Hunting Life: www.foxhuntinglife.com.*

Draft and Driving

Driving is a versatile and fun activity for the home horsekeeper, as it can offer the opportunity for solitary reflection or a social encounter. Children can ride along in the carriage, solving the problem of what to do with the kids while you work your horse. Pleasure driving can be a great way for an older or disabled rider who can no longer ride to stay involved with horses, especially because small ponies or minis can be used for driving and are less physically taxing to care for and handle. Horses can drive alone, in a pair, or in a four-in-hand (or more). The driving experience can range from a casual Sunday drive down rural roads to showing a high-stepping Morgan in fine harness classes to competing in combined driving, which is a high-intensity sport fashioned after eventing that includes dressage, marathon, and cones obstacle phases. One caveat for those considering driving: It requires access to drivable roads and trails. Dirt roads, wide, well-maintained trails, or at least quiet country roads are necessary for driving much more so than for riding.

For a beginning driver, the primary requirement when horse shopping is that the horse is a confirmed, well-trained driving horse. Do not attempt to train your own horse to drive without intense supervision from a professional. Driving can be dangerous, even more so than riding, since there's the potential for a terrible wreck if the horse panics or bolts. So refine your search to horses that have already been trained to drive and have been doing so for several years without incident.

Although virtually any horse can be trained to drive, common breeds for driving include Morgans, Friesians, and any of the draft breeds. Several European warmblood breeds were originally developed as carriage horses. Ponies and miniature horses are also a popular choice for driving, since they are small and low maintenance. Minis and ponies that are much too small for an adult to ride can still easily pull an adult in a cart. In areas where harness racing exists, such as Maine, Ohio, and Florida, retired racing Standardbreds can be retrained as pleasure driving horses. These horses often have stellar temperaments, making them excellent family horses that can serve double duty as trail riding and driving horses.

Ways to Enjoy Your Horse Without Showing

There are lots of ways to get out and about and enjoy a social horse scene without the pressure and anxiety of showing.

Group trail rides are casual events usually planned by a local organization. Riders preregister and arrive at a designated meeting spot, and then the whole group sets off together for a trail ride. Events may include lunch, beach riding, fund-raising for a cause, or other fun activities.

LEFT: Even a small pony can pull adults in a carriage with no difficulty.

RIGHT: A team of mules pulling a carriage.

Riding on the beach is high on the "bucket list" for many horse owners.

Hunter paces are one of my favorite things to do with my horses. A hunter pace is sort of like a group trail ride along a designated route, except that small groups are organized into teams of two or three riders. The event is timed, and may include jumps along the way or not, but generally speaking the level of competition is casual and friendly. Riders can walk, trot, or canter through the countryside, enjoying the scenery and each other's company while "competing" for the chance to earn a prize.

Gymkhanas or game days are another exciting and fun activity. Riders at these events tend to be Western, but English riders are equally welcome. The Pony Club organization also sponsors gymkhana events. These shows feature a variety of fun classes, including pole-bending, barrel racing, flag racing, keyhole racing, and for the kids, egg-and-spoon races, bareback classes, and other games. Technically, a gymkhana or game day is a show, but I included it here because to me it falls into the "fun" category more than the "performance" category.

Clinics are day-long or multi-day intensive classes taught by relatively famous professionals. Participants trailer their horses to the clinic site and participate in one or more sessions, either one-on-one or in a group setting, with the clinician. No matter what discipline you practice, you can probably find a clinic to suit your pleasure.

Some riders who don't have access to regular training or instruction utilize clinics a few times a year to get input from a professional to make sure they're on the right track. This can be a great choice if training options are limited or even nonexistent for your discipline in your area. Others complement their regular lessons with occasional clinics to gain a new perspective. They are also very popular among natural horsemanship practitioners. A clinic can be a great way to gain insight and advance your riding in an intensive, focused environment while also socializing with like-minded equestrians and making contacts in your area—often a vital component of the experience for those of us who keep our horses at home and don't have regular social interactions with other horse people.

Cost to participate varies based on the level of acclaim of the clinician, but they can be quite pricy. A less costly alternative is to attend the clinic as an auditor—that is, as a nonparticipating observer without a horse.

BELOW Many game days include a barrel racing class.

Volunteering at a horse show or other event is a great way to get out there and have some fun without the pressure, stress, or expense of actually showing. Most horse shows are in need of many volunteers to perform such roles as scorer, scribe, jump judge, ring steward, warm-up monitor, bit checker, runner, secretary, and setup and teardown. Even casual events like group trail rides and hunter paces need volunteers to help organize, check in riders, mark trail routes, and other tasks. The benefit to you is that you'll be able to interact with other riders and be part of the "scene," while supporting a good cause. Most of these types of events would not be able to survive without volunteers.

Scribing at dressage shows is one of my favorite activities. The scribe gets to sit beside the judge and watch every test, while writing down the judge's scores and comments for each movement. This alone is a fabulous learning opportunity, and the scribe also has the chance to meet the judges as well as all the competitors in the area. During times when I've been unable to ride enough to justify showing, such as when I'm pregnant or have a newborn, scribing is a great outlet for my horse passion. I get to stay involved and keep my hand in the horsey scene without having to ride or deal with the stress of show prep.

6. Types of Horses and What to Look For

Breeds

THERE ARE LITERALLY hundreds of horse breeds across the globe. A multitude of books focusing on horse breeds will show you photos and describe a vast array of horses. Here I've selected the most common pleasure horse breeds in North America, the ones most often owned by amateur horse owners.

American Quarter Horses, Appaloosas, and Paints

The American Quarter Horse is the most common horse breed in the United States. Originally developed for working on cattle ranches, these horses are typically quiet, intelligent, and trainable, making them nearly an ideal choice for the novice or amateur rider. Note that there are now many different types of Quarter Horses being bred for many different purposes. For riding, you'll want a performance type rather than a halter type.

The Quarter Horse traditionally belongs to the Western disciplines—it is the rodeo cowboy's horse, the barrel racer, the gaming horse, the roper, the trail horse, the Western pleasure show horse. However, their sheer numbers, popularity, and versatility mean they are also commonly found in the hunter or dressage arenas. You'll often find Quarter Horse crosses mixed with Arabian, Thorough-

The American Quarter Horse is an ideal pleasure mount.

bred, and draft bloodlines. *American Quarter Horse Association: www. aqha.org.*

I include Paints and Appaloosas with Quarter Horses because they are all considered stock horse breeds—the traditionally Western breeds—and all have a high percentage of Quarter Horse blood. Paints have similar characteristics to Quarter Horses, but with the distinctive white-painted coat colors. (A "breeding stock" Paint is a horse with Paint bloodlines that does not happen to have the white markings. Note also that *Paint* is a breed, registered with the American Paint Horse Association, while *pinto* is a color designation for a white-splattered coat pattern that can be found in horses of many breeds.) *American Paint Horse Association: www.apha.com.*

BELOW: American Paint Horses.

BELOW: The distinctive "blanket" coat pattern of the Appaloosa.

Appaloosas are a stock horse breed that features another unique coat color pattern, with smaller spots either throughout the coat or concentrated in a blanket over the rump. Distinctive of the Appaloosas are their striped hooves and mottled noses. Appaloosas are known for being hardy, intelligent, and stubborn. *Appaloosa Horse Club: www.appaloosa.com.*

Arabians

Arabians are extremely popular as pleasure and trail horses, and can be found competing in both Western and English disciplines. They are one of the oldest breeds of horses, and many modern breeds can be traced back to an Arabian heritage, including Thoroughbreds, warmbloods, and Quarter Horses. They are willing, versatile, people-oriented partners, and are generally hardy and easy to maintain. They excel at the disciplines of endurance and competitive trail riding due to their stamina and resilience. They're a smallish breed of horse, commonly ranging from 14 to 15.2 hands, but they tend to be strong enough to carry heavier riders anyway. Many believe Arabians to be the most beautiful of all horse breeds.

One caveat is that they may be more spirited, hotter, and spookier than some other breeds, so depending on the temperament of the specific horse, they may be harder for a novice rider to handle and ride.

ABOVE: Arabian horse. (Note that the T-posts in the background should be capped for safety.)

ABOVE: A stunning Arabian-Paint cross.

They are also very sensitive and intelligent, so beginners may find themselves outsmarted by their own horse. As always, when horse-shopping, assess each animal as an individual, but keep the breed characteristics in the back of your mind.

Another option is to seek out a half-Arabian. Arabians are often crossed with other breeds in an effort to bring lightness, stamina, and elegance to a heavier breed. Arab-Quarter Horses, Arab-Thoroughbreds (technically called Anglo-Arabs), and Arab-Saddlebreds (called National Show Horses) are common. *Arabian Horse Association: www.arabianhorses.org.*

Drafts and Draft Crosses

Draft horses, as the name makes clear, comprise the heavy horse breeds originally developed for use on farms and for driving. As such, riding is not their intended use, and many may be too heavy or not well built for riding. However, some draft horses with lighter

LEFT: This Belgian draft horse is not especially well suited to riding. Her heavy build, straight back, and low withers will make saddle fitting difficult, while her steep croup, straight stifle, and rather upright shoulder make her gait short, choppy, and earthbound. Her very short, thick neck and short back will make it hard for her to flex, bend, and accept the bridle.

RIGHT: Although the same breed as the horse in the previous photo, this Belgian mare's conformation makes her much more appropriate for riding. She has a much lighter build, with a graceful neck, sloping shoulder, round hindquarters, and a longer back. Her conformation is not perfect, but she looks like an excellent partner for pleasure riding.

conformation can make excellent riding horses, and their calm and willing dispositions make them ideal for timid or beginning riders. Some breeds commonly used in the United States for riding as well as driving are Percherons, Belgians, Shires, and Clydesdales.

In addition, draft crosses are becoming extremely popular as pleasure and dressage mounts. These are draft-breed horses crossed with a lighter saddle-horse breed, usually Thoroughbred, but sometimes Quarter Horse, warmblood, Arabian, or another light breed. Belgian-Thoroughbred and Percheron-Thoroughbred are especially nice crosses. In a good cross, you'll get the sturdiness and temperament of the draft horse combined with the lightness of bone and athleticism of the Thoroughbred. *Belgian Draft Horse Corporation of America: www.belgiancorp.com. Percheron Horse Association of America: www.percheronhorse.org. Clydesdale Breeders of the USA: http://clydeusa. com. American Shire Horse Association: www.shirehorse.com.*

Gaited Breeds

"Gaited" means having an extra natural gait in addition to the usual walk, trot, and canter. This extra gait is usually a smooth, fast, easy-to-ride alternative to the trot. For example, Saddlebreds have the rack and Tennessee Walking Horses, the running walk. Other common gaited breeds are Rocky Mountain Horses, Standardbreds,

BELOW: Clydesdale horses in harness.

BELOW: Peruvian Paso horse performing its lateral gait, the paso llano.

Missouri Fox Trotters, Paso Finos, and Icelandics. Many of these breeds compete on their own breed show circuits or in saddleseat competition, but they are also good trail mounts. The breeds were specifically developed for trail and pleasure riding, and are gaining in popularity among older adult pleasure riders, since their smooth gaits are much easier to ride for people with arthritis or bad backs. They're generally not the best choice for dressage or hunter/jumper riders, since some may have difficulty trotting and cantering instead of performing their usual gait. *Gaited Horses: www.gaitedhorses.net.*

Grade Horses

A "grade" horse is simply an unregistered horse of unknown breeding—the mutt of the horse world. These horses are widely available, generally inexpensive, and often an excellent choice for a first-time horse owner. Simply due to the widespread popularity of Quarter Horses in the United States, many grade horses are unregistered Quarter Horses or Quarter Horse-type. Draft crosses and Thoroughbred crosses are also common. One thing to watch out for when considering a grade horse is its conformation. Since these horses are not registered or approved by any breed organization, it's reasonable to conclude that the sire and dam may have been an accidental pairing, or one made with less than rigorous criteria. As such, the parents may be poorly matched, or worse, poorly conformed themselves. Read the section below on conformation, and carefully assess your prospect with long-term soundness in mind.

Morgans

The Morgan is an American breed that originated with one specific stallion—Figure, also called "Justin Morgan's horse"—in Vermont in the 1700s. Morgans are a very typey breed, easily identi-

fied by their sturdy appearance, arching necks, distinctive heads, and long manes and tails. They are not especially tall, usually 15 to 16 hands, are usually bay or dark brown, and are most common in New England, their place of origin. Their friendly and sensible dispositions make them excellent trail and pleasure mounts. They are often used for driving as well as riding, and may be seen in lower-level dressage competition as well. *American Morgan Horse Association: www.morganhorse.com.*

Ponies and Minis

There are a variety of pony breeds of varying size and type. Shetlands, Welsh ponies, and Pony of the Americas tend to be the right size for children. Shetlands are very small, and are known for their devious nature, but many an adult rider has fond memories of the devilish little Shetland pony they had as a child. They come in two main types—classic and modern. Classic Shetlands are shaggy and stocky, while modern Shetlands are refined and slender, appearing more like tiny horses than ponies.

Welsh ponies are, simply put, adorable. They range in size, with four different categories. Welsh section A ponies (Welsh mountain ponies) are the smallest at no larger than 12.2 hands; section B ponies are mid-sized at up to 13.2 hands; section C (Welsh pony of cob type) are also up to 13.2 hands, but are less refined than section B ponies; and section D (Welsh cobs) can be quite large, even horse-sized, with no upper height limit. Section C and D ponies and cobs are often used for driving as well as riding. Many show ponies in all disciplines are Welsh. *Welsh Pony & Cob Society: www.welshpony.org.*

Pony of the Americas (POA) is a unique breed that looks like a small Appaloosa. Originated by the accidental breeding of a Shetland stallion and an Arabian/Appaloosa mare, the POA was then developed into a breed in its own right. Ranging from 11 to 14 hands, they make great kids' ponies, despite the fact that they can be a little stubborn, like their larger spotted cousins. POAs are commonly seen in the show ring in both Western and English disciplines. *Pony of the Americas Club, Inc.: www.poac.org.*

Pony breeds that can sometimes be larger and therefore suitable for older children or small adults are Connemaras, Haflingers, Quarter Ponies (undersized Quarter Horses), and German riding ponies. The German riding pony is relatively new on the American scene, and is basically a pint-sized warmblood, with the athletic conformation and powerful gaits of a full-sized warmblood in a smaller package. The Haflinger is a draft-type pony resembling a small Belgian horse. They

BELOW: Classic Shetland pony.

BELOW: Welsh ponies are a common sight in the hunter show ring.

may be used as driving ponies, but their stellar dispositions make them equally well suited as children's mounts. The Connemara is a large pony breed of Irish origin that excels in eventing and dressage.

Miniature horses are an extremely small breed of horse developed from Falabella and Shetland ponies. Most are too small for riding of any kind, although some are large enough for very young children to ride. Miniatures are best suited for driving or as companions. They are a great choice for an older owner who may find them physically easier to handle and care for, while still reaping the emotional benefits of horse ownership. An owner with only one riding horse may choose to add a miniature horse as a low-cost, low-maintenance companion. *American Miniature Horse Association: www. amha.org.*

ABOVE: Three Haflinger ponies.

Keep in mind that although minis and ponies are smaller and certainly do eat much less than a large horse, their hoof care and veterinary costs will be the same. An additional concern with minis as well as small ponies is their tendency toward obesity and laminitis. A common saying among knowledgeable horsemen is that there are only two types of ponies: those that have foundered, and those that will founder. This may be an exaggeration, but it highlights the fact that smaller equines generally can't safely be kept on grass pastures full-time, nor allowed unlimited access to hay. If you keep your horses on pasture or feed round bales, think carefully before adding a mini or small pony to your herd. You'll need to consider dry-lotting

LEFT: Minis in a driving class.
CREDIT: *SF photo / Shutterstock.com*

the pony to limit his access to grass, or using a grazing muzzle so he can't vacuum up the grass as quickly.

Thoroughbreds

Because the racing industry produces around 30,000 Thoroughbred foals each year, retired off-the-track racehorses are plentiful and easy to come by. Race trainers sell horses who are not working out as racehorses, generally because they're just too slow, but sometimes because they've been injured or are older. It is possible to buy them directly from racetracks or racing trainers if you are confident in your ability to train and handle a young horse. There are several organizations that exist to facilitate this process, including CANTER (www.canterusa.org), New Vocations (www.horseadoption.com), and ReRun (www.rerun.org). If you're not an experienced rider, it's best to look for a horse that has been off the track for several years and has been retrained by a competent trainer.

Many people believe that all Thoroughbreds are "hot" and spirited. This certainly can be the case. However, as with most stereotypes, it's not always true. Many Thoroughbreds turn out to be wonderful, calm, intelligent, people-oriented horses. This is another reason it's best to seek out a Thoroughbred who has already been retrained as a riding horse—you can assess his personality as a pleasure horse much more easily than one that is still racing-fit at the track.

Thoroughbreds make excellent all-around horses for trail and pleasure riding, but they especially excel at the English disciplines—eventing, dressage, and hunter/jumper. *The Jockey Club: www.jockey club.com. Thoroughbred Owners and Breeders Association: www.toba.org.*

Warmbloods

Warmblood is not a breed of horse, but rather a type. Warmbloods are sport horses selectively bred in Europe over many generations, to result in the gorgeous, athletic, big-moving dressage horses and jumpers we know today. There are many individual warmblood regis-

ABOVE Thoroughbreds are often athletic jumpers.

tries, including Dutch warmbloods, Swedish warmbloods, Holsteiners, Hanoverians, and Trakehners. The term "American warmblood" is sometimes used to refer to generically bred sport-type horses or to draft crosses, but more correctly means a horse registered with the American Warmblood Society or American Warmblood Registry. (The word "warmblood" originated as a reference to the blend of "hot blooded" horses—Thoroughbreds and Arabians—with "cold blooded" horses—drafts—in their ancestry. Today, though, that meaning has largely been attenuated as warmbloods have become a recognized type in their own right and are no longer literally a cross between hot- and cold-blooded horses.)

A warmblood is an excellent choice for a rider looking to excel at dressage or one of the jumping disciplines. They do tend to be expensive—price should be reflective of quality—so a casual trail or pleasure rider may be able to find a better trained, more appropriate horse at a lower price by choosing a nonwarmblood breed.

Temperament

When selecting a pleasure horse for a novice or amateur owner, temperament is perhaps the single most important factor. The horse can be the most poorly conformed beast on the planet, of a breed unsuited to the rider's chosen discipline, and unpleasant in color, but if he's got a great mind, nobody's going to get hurt and the pair will probably have fun, too. (One exception to this rule is jumping. A horse that is physically unsuited to jumping can be unsafe—if he can't get himself and his rider over the jumps correctly, there's increased risk of a fall.)

Look for a horse that's calm and quiet but attentive on the ground. Regardless of age, any horse worth his salt should lead and tie well, stand calmly and patiently until asked to move, and should walk and trot in hand at the handler's shoulder without crowding the handler, lagging behind, or dragging ahead.

When you ride the horse, be alert for tension, spookiness, balkiness, or a tendency to get quick. Regardless of discipline, any well-trained horse should be attentive and responsive to your aids. An ideal beginner's horse is forgiving of rookie rider mistakes and will try his best to figure out what you want, even if you're not quite asking correctly. This is where temperament becomes crucial. Some horses get angry

RIGHT: For an all-around family horse, temperament is the most important consideration.

when their riders make mistakes, and they may develop bad habits like bucking, rearing, or balking. Others get confused and upset. Others are smarter and quickly realize that they can take advantage of their riders, and will develop evasions like getting quick, popping a shoulder, or spooking at nothing. The best horses are tolerant and patient, and will stay quiet and willing under almost any circumstances.

If you're planning to trail ride (and most people who keep their horses at home do), make sure your potential horse is calm and safe on trails, both alone and with companions. A horse who is barn sour or buddy sour, or who becomes a spooky, frantic mess on the trail, is no fun and can be dangerous, and will sharply limit your riding options once you get him home. Not all horses are cut out to be trail horses—and yours should be.

Soundness

The second priority after temperament is soundness. Obviously, if you're planning to ride, soundness is very important. Why do I place it second and not first? Because *any* horse you buy can later become unsound. Would you rather be stuck with a nutty, high-strung, hard-to-handle lame horse, or a calm, pleasant, companionable lame horse? See my point?

Now, keep in mind that there are degrees of unsoundness. There are many horses out there who are "pasture sound"—that is, they look just fine walking and trotting around the pasture with their buddies and show no sign of being in pain. However, they can't be ridden because when put to work under saddle, their underlying unsoundness appears. These types of horses are ideal as companions, and they can often be acquired for free, since they're not useful as riding horses.

Another level of soundness is the horse that can no longer comfortably perform in its former competitive discipline—be it reining, dressage, or jumping—due to injury or simply old age, but is still quite sound for lower level riding or casual trail riding. Some horses that

LEFT: When assessing a horse's soundness, a vet may perform a flexion test—bending the horse's joints for several seconds before asking the horse to trot off quickly, which will exacerbate any subtle unsoundness.

are considered "unsound" when competing at 3'6" jumpers or fourth-level dressage are perfectly fine to jump 2 feet or ride training level dressage. And some horses that can't perform even at that level may be capable of doing easy walk-trot trail rides on the weekends. So when assessing soundness with your vet, keep in mind your riding goals for the horse. Of course, it's ideal to find a perfectly sound horse. But you may be able to offer a great home to a nice quality horse who needs to step down a level or two in performance due to his soundness. Be sure to keep in mind the horse's likely future soundness—many conditions, such as navicular disease or arthritis, are degenerative, and the horse will probably continue to decline with age.

Going hand in hand with soundness is maintenance. Does the horse need daily supplements, special shoeing, joint injections, or other considerations to keep him comfortable? Take into account the expense of these requirements. They may not be deal-breakers for you, but it's important to know all of the factors when making your purchasing decision.

When assessing any potential horse, always, always, always get a prepurchase exam from a veterinarian, regardless of the purchase price of the horse. The prepurchase exam should alert you to any underlying physical issues that the horse may have. A vet bill down the road for a $500 trail horse is going to be just as costly as one for a $20,000 jumper. See the section in chapter 7 on The Prepurchase Exam for a full discussion of the topic.

Conformation

Conformation is the way a horse's body is shaped—the way it is conformed. A horse with excellent conformation will be able to use his body more easily and fluidly, and will be less prone to lameness due to injuries and joint degeneration. However, for a family pleasure mount, conformation is lower in importance than temperament and soundness. Barring extreme deviations from the norm, a horse with imperfect conformation and a stellar personality is a much better choice than one with ideal conformation and a sour or rank disposition. That being said, conformation is certainly a large piece of the horse-shopping puzzle, so it's important to understand the basics.

Each breed and discipline favors slightly different aspects of conformation, and there are so many subtleties that conformation analysis is a complex science as well as an art. I don't expect you to learn every detail of conformation analysis. But when assessing any horse you're considering, you'll need to take a close look at the following major points:

1. Overall impression. Stand back and take in the horse as a unit, viewing from the side. Does he seem balanced? Is his head too large for his body? Do his hindquarters look weak and underdeveloped? Is his back very long? Does he appear athletic and fit, or weak and lanky? In general, you'll want to steer clear of a horse

RIGHT: Stand back and assess your overall impression of the horse. This warmblood is somewhat undermuscled, but his overall conformation is good, with straight, clean legs, good pastern length, a decent shoulder angle, and a level (if not uphill) build. On the negative side, he is long in the back and lanky, with a weak-looking neck and hindquarters.

that appears to be made up of parts from several different animals. His anatomy should appear seamless and well balanced. He should "fit in a box" with a length from chest to tail that is approximately the same as the height from hoof to withers.

2. Uphill vs. downhill build. Again viewing from the side, does the horse's body appear to be sloping downward from hips to shoulders, or upward? Are his withers even with the point of hip, or higher or lower? Similarly, compare the level of the stifle to elbow and hock to knee. For many Western disciplines, a slight downhill build is acceptable. But for virtually all English disciplines, you'll have an easier time with a horse that's built uphill or at least level along his topline. The withers should be slightly higher than the hip, and the elbow slightly higher than or level with the stifle. This conformation gives a horse a natural ability to collect, lift his front end, and carry more weight on the hind end—a virtual necessity for dressage or jumping.

3. Front legs. As the base of the horse's skeletal system, the legs are of great importance for long-term soundness. Viewed from the side, the front legs should appear plumb and straight along the fronts. A horse who is "over at the knee" or "back at the knee" (with his knees slightly ahead of or behind an imaginary vertical line) may have soundness issues later in life. The pasterns of all four legs should be gently sloping with good length. Short, upright pasterns suggest a choppy, jarring stride that's uncomfortable to ride. Pasterns

LEFT: This Lusitano is of a very different type than the first horse we looked at. He is beautiful, with a compact build, a short back, and a good amount of bone—meaning his legs look proportional to his body rather than being too thin and frail. However, his short, upright pasterns, straight hind limb angles, and nearly vertical shoulder angle suggest that his stride will be choppy, with an up-and-down "sewing machine" action.

that are excessively long and sloping may be weak, predisposing the horse to soft-tissue injuries. As a rule of thumb, the angle of the pastern should match the angle of the front of the hoof. Carefully run your hands down the legs, looking for any lumps, bumps, swelling, or scarring that could indicate prior injury. Next stand in front of the horse and assess his legs from the front. Again, they should look straight and true, neither bowed out nor in and neither twisted to the outside or inside.

4. Hind legs. The hind legs should be well angled through the stifle and hock joints. If they're too straight, the horse will move with a shorter stride and may be more prone to unsoundness. The pasterns should match the angle of the front pasterns, as well as the angle of the hoof. The hocks and cannon bones of the hind legs should not be "slung under" the horse's body at an angle (sickle-hocked), nor camped out behind the horse—the cannons should be right under the hips and nearly perpendicular to the ground. Stand behind the horse and make sure he's not cow-hocked, with hocks that are pointing toward each other and toes that point out dramatically. Again, viewed from behind the legs should be straight, although the toes may point outward slightly.

5. Shoulder and withers. The shoulder should be nicely sloped from the withers to the chest. A shoulder that's too vertical will result in a choppy, bouncy stride and limited range of motion in the front limbs. The withers should be well developed. Flat, "mutton" withers may make saddle fitting difficult, as will extremely high, narrow "shark fin" withers.

6. Neck and head. Look for an elegant, well formed neck with a slight convex arch along the topline. A horse that is ewe-necked (with a concave arch) will find it difficult to round his topline and accept the bridle. The ideal head is in good proportion to the neck and body, and has large eyes and nostrils. The eye should appear soft and intelligent. Try not to focus too much on an adorable face, since its cuteness may distract you from serious conformation flaws elsewhere.

7. Back and hindquarters. These should appear strong and toned. Avoid a horse with a swayback, as this can indicate weakness and will at minimum make saddle fitting a chore. The back should be a length that's in good proportion to the rest of the body, erring on the side of too short rather than too long. The hindquarters should be muscular and round; look out for the telltale bump at the top of the hip that can indicate sacroiliac injury.

As you can see, there's a lot to consider, and I've only touched the surface here. Keep in mind that no horse has perfect conformation, so don't get too wrapped up in the search for the ideal. Especially for a pleasure or trail horse, a minor conformation flaw is perfectly fine, as long as the horse is sound (see The Prepurchase Exam in chapter 7). The most important point to consider is the legs. Clean, straight legs are a very good sign. A major flaw, inconsistency, or injury to the legs may be a deal-breaker.

Age and Training

Age and training level of the horse are important considerations, but what to look for depends heavily on your experience and expectations. For the majority of amateur riders, a middle-aged, well-trained horse is going to provide the most satisfaction. Look for a horse between eight and twelve years old. At this age, the horse will have grown out of his youthful sillies and should have quite a bit of training and life experience, but still has a lot of sound, healthy years left in his body.

Make sure he has at least some training and experience in your chosen discipline. A horse intended for trail or pleasure riding should have trail riding experience, so you don't have to be the one to train him to cross water, follow patiently or lead confidently, and not spook at fallen logs and fluttering leaves. A horse intended for lower-level dressage does not need to be showing at an upper level, but it will be easier for the rider to learn and move up the levels on a mount with show experience who is trained to at least first level. If you want a partner to compete at gaming or gymkhana shows, look for a horse that knows how to run barrels and poles and has seen a cow or two in her day. The bottom line is, you will probably have more fun with a horse that knows his job, so you are not struggling constantly with training hurdles at even the most basic level.

For a more advanced rider looking for a project, a younger, greener horse can be a good choice. Many riders derive much pleasure from training young horses. If you are one of these riders, you probably already know it, and you know what to look for. It takes an experienced eye to see potential in a young, still-growing horse, and it's something that can't be taught in a book. Again, it comes down to temperament, soundness, and conformation.

When you're first starting out, I advise against buying a baby. Unless you know how to handle youngsters, they can quickly develop bad habits and become unmanageable. Even on the ground, they need consistent, gentle yet firm, daily handling from an experienced handler so they grow up learning to be polite, respectful horses. Yes, you can buy a much higher quality horse for much less money if you buy a youngster. But when it comes time to start that baby, you will most likely need to pay for professional training, which is expensive and will eat up all of your imagined "savings." Don't buy anything younger than four years old, and don't buy anything that hasn't been started, going walk, trot, and canter under saddle.

Another fallacy among novice horse owners is that it is fun to buy a young pony for a child and let them "grow up together." This plan is dangerous and ill advised. It's far better for your child to learn on an elderly, been-there-done-that pony that will keep her safe and teach her how to ride.

In fact, for young children or for riders looking for a calm, quiet trail partner, a senior horse may be the way to go. A horse over sixteen years old is likely to be much quieter and less prone to sudden outbursts than a younger horse, and will keep children and timid riders safe. As always, this is a stereotype and is not always true, but in general an older horse has a better chance of being a safe and steady mount. Most horses remain sound for riding well into their twenties, and ponies even into their thirties.

Size

The size of a horse is not hugely important, as long as the horse is able to carry its intended rider with ease. Even a short horse, if he's strong and stocky with a short, well-muscled back, can carry a heavier rider. The rule of thumb is that the maximum amount a horse should be expected to carry is 20 percent of his own weight, including tack. Thus, the average 1,000-pound horse should be capable of carrying up to 200 pounds of rider and saddle. Very heavy riders will want to take care to choose a horse that's appropriate both in terms of size and weight-carrying ability. A close-coupled, compact horse may be better equipped to handle a rider's weight than a horse with a long back and weedy conformation.

Of course, a very tall rider might not want to consider shorter horses, simply because he or she may feel awkward on a mismatched horse. Don't discount a horse based on height alone, however. A small horse with a large barrel can take up more of the rider's leg than a tall horse of slender build.

In general, daily care and handling can be easier with a somewhat smaller horse. Trail riders may want to take into consideration the ease of mounting a 15-hand horse as opposed to a 17-hand horse, since there are no mounting blocks in the middle of the woods.

Gender

Horses come in three gender options—mare, stallion, and gelding (a castrated male). (There are also spayed mares, but these are extremely rare, as spaying is an invasive surgery used only in cases of health problems or severe behavioral issues stemming from hormones.) For novice horse owners, the only reasonable options are mares and geldings. Stallions, with their excess of testosterone, are not a good choice for beginners, as they require specialized care and handling to make sure they stay safe and well behaved. There's also the inherent risk of them escaping and breeding neighboring mares. Geldings tend to be much more tractable than either stallions or mares. Mares may be more opinionated and sensitive than geldings, and some can be prone to cyclical hormonal fluctuations as they come into heat, making them irritable. There is an old saying among horsemen that highlights their temperamental differences: "Tell a gelding, ask a mare, discuss it with a stallion."

That having been said, each horse is an individual. My gelding, Beamer, is extremely opinionated and sensitive, and requires firm handling and a tactful rider. My trainer has mentioned that he seems "more like a stallion or a mare" than a gelding. The mares, Robin and Allegro, are the most even-tempered horses at my barn. Therefore, I put gender low on the list of considerations when horse-shopping. As long as you avoid stallions and keep in mind the individual characteristics of the mares and geldings you consider, gender is not a deal-breaker.

Color

The old saying is true—a good horse is never a bad color. Of all the possible considerations when horse-shopping, color is lowest on the list. Of course, I understand that you may have your fantasy horse in mind—a black stallion, a gorgeous dapple gray, a blood bay with a blaze and four white stockings. I myself have always coveted a tricolor paint. And I'm not saying that you can't look for that dream horse. What I am saying is that it should not be your primary criterion. Don't overlook the perfect horse because he's not the color you want, and by all means, do *not* buy an inappropriate horse because his color is pretty. Gorgeous coloring can sometimes distract our eye from bad conformation. Picture what that flashy horse would look like as a plain bay. Do you still like him? If so, great! Snap him up! If not, well, you have your answer.

7. Horse Shopping

Shopping Online

THERE ARE MANY, many online horse sales sites these days. There are discipline- or breed-specific sites, as well as general sites like Equine.com or Dreamhorse.com. These sites are great for brainstorming, inspiration, and getting a sense of the market in your area. They also allow you to search for horses outside your local area. Most sites have advanced search functions that allow you to tailor your search by price, breed, height, age, gender, geographic location, discipline, or even level of training of the horse. You can get a good sense of each horse through descriptions, photos, and even videos online.

Once you've found a horse, or a selection of horses, that interests you, call or email the listed buyer with questions. Make sure your questions are relevant to the specific horse and your specific needs, and have not already been answered in the ad. For example, don't ask if the horse has been started over fences if the ad clearly states the horse is jumping 2-foot courses. This kind of behavior only serves to annoy the seller and portrays you as a foolish or un-serious buyer. The seller may also have questions for you about your experience, intentions, and plans for the horse. Most sellers care about their horses and want to be sure the new home is a good match.

Steps in the Horse Buying Process

1. Find a horse—through your trainer, through advertising sources such as print or online classifieds, or by word of mouth.
2. Contact the seller and ask questions. Answer any that the seller has for you.
3. Schedule a visit to try the horse. Bring your trainer. If you like the horse, be prepared to make an offer and put down a deposit.
4. Schedule a prepurchase exam with your veterinarian.
5. If the horse passes the prepurchase exam, bring him home!

How to Find Horses for Sale

Online sales sites

Print magazines or local horsey newsletters with classified sections

Through your trainer—her professional contacts may be an excellent resource.

Word of mouth—ask around at horse shows and through all your local horse contacts, such as your vet, farrier, and friends. Let everyone know what you're looking for.

Riding stables—inquire at local riding stables for lesson horses that are no longer able to stand up to the rigors of their professional lives, but might make good prospects for backyard trail horses.

Sale barns and dealers—tread carefully here, as dealers are in it for the bottom line rather than for the best interests of horses and clients. Bring a trainer or knowledgeable friend, and insist on a prepurchase exam.

Once you've established communication with the seller, have had all your questions answered, and are confident that this horse merits further consideration, set up a visit.

The Role of the Trainer

It's generally best to work with your own trainer or riding instructor when looking for a horse to buy, especially if you're a novice at horse ownership. Your trainer knows your riding ability better than anyone else, and can screen out unsuitable horses. She has a much more experienced eye for horseflesh and soundness (that's why she makes the big bucks, right?) and may have leads on potential horses being sold by other trainers in the area.

Have your trainer help you review any "horse for sale" ads you find, and plan to have your trainer accompany you on any visits. Depending on your own level of competence, you may want to make an initial visit on your own and then bring the trainer along for the second trip if you like the horse. The trainer can ride the horse herself or just watch you ride and offer advice or opinions. Ultimately, your trainer's level of involvement is up to you. Some buyers simply give their trainer a free hand to find, select, and buy a new horse for them. Most buyers, however, want to be the leader in the selection process, bringing the trainer in as a consultant before making a final decision.

Typically, after a successful purchase the buyer compensates the trainer for her assistance with 10 percent of the purchase price of the horse. Be sure you discuss your trainer's expectations for compensation before embarking on your horse search with her.

Trying a Horse

When you go to try out a horse, request that the owner not groom and tack up for you. Doing these tasks yourself will give you a good sense of the horse's overall attitude. Does he flinch or shy when you brush his head? Does he kick out when you touch his flanks or belly? Does he dance around while you position the saddle? Does he pin his ears or threaten to bite when you tighten the girth? All of these are red flags indicating poor training or rough handling, a bad attitude, lack of respect, or in some cases a potential physical problem. You want a horse that stands quietly and patiently while being groomed and tacked, that lets you touch any part of his body and picks up his hooves when asked, and that accepts the saddle and bridle willingly and without a fuss.

Before riding, lead the horse around for a bit and assess his attitude toward you. Is he attentive and ready for your cues? Does he lead well and stand at the mounting block? Will he back up, turn in both directions, and trot in hand with subtle cues?

If the horse knows how to longe, ask the seller to demonstrate this for you. Note the horse's attitude and attentiveness to the handler. Does he respond promptly to verbal cues to walk, trot, canter, and whoa? Does he show any fear of the whip or aggressiveness toward the handler? Now is also a good time to assess the horse's gaits, with an eye toward the requirements of your chosen discipline.

Never be the first one to ride a potential horse. Always ask the owner or the owner's trainer to ride first. (If the seller refuses to get on the horse—this is a major red flag!) If all goes well, try him yourself. Always ride in an arena or enclosed area when you're on an unfamiliar horse. Note whether the horse stands calmly and patiently at the mounting block, or if he needs to be held. Walk, trot, and canter or lope in both directions. Try several changes of direction at the walk and trot. Does the horse move forward willingly and slow down easily when asked? Does he respond well to leg and seat aids? Are his gaits comfortable and balanced?

If you're considering this horse for a specific discipline, be sure to put him to the test. Try cantering a jump, or even a small course, if you'll be jumping the horse at home. For a dressage prospect, note whether the horse willingly goes on the bit and bends his body in response to light leg and seat aids. For a speed or barrel horse, can he quickly accelerate while staying in control? If you're planning to trail

LEFT: Tack up the horse yourself to get a sense of his temperament and ground manners.

ride, ask if there's somewhere you can take the horse for a little test ride down the trail. The seller may wish to accompany you on another horse.

One of the most important considerations for a first-time or novice owner is the horse's temperament and behavior under saddle. He should remain calm, willing, and responsive. He should be tolerant of rider errors, rather than becoming anxious or irritable. Pinning ears and a swishing tail are signs of resistance that could indicate either an attitude problem or a physical problem, such as back pain. Obviously, such forms of resistance as bucking, kicking out, rearing, or balking are to be avoided. In theory, a good trainer can help you work through some of these problems—but wouldn't it be better to buy a horse without training problems in the first place? One vice that is an absolute deal-breaker is rearing. Not the little bunny-hop type of rearing, but full-blown vertical rearing. This is extremely danger-

RIGHT: Try to get a sense of whether you "click" with this particular horse— whether you will truly love riding him every day.

ous, as the horse can easily flip over backward, either by accident or deliberately, potentially resulting in severe injury or even death to the rider or himself. I would also consider rank bucking to be a deal-breaker. Again, a little resistance in the form of a crow hop is not a death sentence for an otherwise nice horse, but if you find a horse that goes into rodeo mode and is deliberately trying to ditch the rider, pass.

Making an Offer

After riding the horse, you may decide to go try a few others before making a final decision. You can also ask the seller if you can schedule a second visit to ride the horse again. Realize that the seller has no obligation to hold the horse for you at this point, so he may be sold to someone else if you wait and come back later. Nevertheless, buying a horse is a major life decision, so you should not let anyone pressure you into making a choice before you're 100 percent sure.

When you are confident that this is the horse for you, make an offer to the seller, contingent on a prepurchase exam. The seller may accept, reject, or counter-offer. (Note that these proceedings may be handled by your trainer acting as your agent, if you've authorized her to do so.) Once the seller has accepted your offer, you may be asked to put down a deposit. This is a good-faith payment to the seller so she can take the horse off the market with confidence that you will not disappear into the night, and you can be confident that the seller will hold the horse for you until you can schedule a prepurchase exam.

In some cases, the seller may offer a short-term trial period—from a week to a month or so—for you to take the horse home, ride him, and get to know him before making a final decision. If you decide to go this route, be sure to get everything in writing so there are no mis-understandings. The horse should be insured (by you) so that if any accident befalls him, the seller is covered. The prepurchase exam can take place during the trial period as well.

The Prepurchase Exam

Once you've chosen a horse that you're seriously interested in buying, the next step is to arrange a prepurchase exam with a veterinarian. Don't use the seller's vet, who may be biased. Use your own vet or an independent vet. Perform a prepurchase exam on *any* horse you're looking to buy. It may feel odd to spend $200 on an exam for a $500 horse, but remember that if that horse turns out to be unsound, you're going to have to spend lots more than that on veterinary costs in the future. A thorough prepurchase exam can save you a lot of heartache (and wallet ache) down the road.

The veterinarian will perform a thorough exam on the horse, looking for unsoundness or potential health problems that may crop up later in life. Explain to the vet your intended use for the horse, as a horse that is sound for light trail riding may not be the same as a

BELOW: In addition to assessing soundness, the vet will perform an overall check of the horse's health.

ABOVE: The vet will discuss with you the findings of her prepurchase exam, including any concerns or recommended further testing.

horse that is sound for jumping. Depending on your desires (and how much money you're willing to spend on the exam) the vet may recommend further testing, such as X-rays or blood tests.

Depending on what he finds the vet may not give the horse a "pass" or "fail" on the exam, but should present you with an overview of potential issues and discuss with you the implications of his findings. It is then up to you as a buyer to decide whether you still want to buy the horse, not buy the horse, or perhaps submit a revised offer to the seller. (For example, if an X-ray reveals a previously unknown bone chip that needs surgery but the horse will then be sound, you may want to make a lower offer reflecting the increased costs associated with buying the horse.)

Should I Rescue a Horse?

As a first-time horse owner, the short answer to this question may be "No, you should not." It can make us feel good inside

Rules of Thumb for Horse Shopping

- Never buy the first horse you see.
- A good horse is never a bad color.
- Always get a prepurchase exam.
- Be honest about your level of experience—don't buy more horse than you can handle.

to remove a horse from a bad home and give it a second chance at a happy life. However, many rescued horses have come from abusive or neglectful situations and need specialized care and handling from an experienced owner. But there is more than one way to "rescue" a horse, and adopting from a reputable horse rescue society may work out extremely well for you. These groups do all the groundwork for you, locating horses in need, carrying out any needed medical treatments and bringing the horse back to good condition, and possibly doing ridden assessments and some training as well. Working with an established rescue group can offer you the satisfaction of knowing you're helping a horse in need—and making room for the rescue to take in another horse—while preventing you from getting in over your head with a starved or traumatized horse.

If you're considering rescuing a horse, the information below can help you choose the ideal route for you.

Buying from an Auction

The slaughter of horses for human consumption is a contentious issue in the United States right now. Legislation is going back and forth on whether or not it is legal. Regardless, many auctions do sell horses to "kill buyers" who ship them to Canada and Mexico for slaughter. Therefore, buying a horse at an auction that would otherwise ship to slaughter is a way to save that horse from an extremely unpleasant journey and a grisly demise. However, buying at auction is extremely risky. Do not consider an auction to be a way to acquire a horse cheaply. Yes, the purchase price may be relatively low, but since the horse's history is unknown, you may be faced with expensive vet bills or training costs if the horse is ill, lame, rank, or poorly trained. Horses at auctions are generally sold with no guarantees for soundness or temperament. In addition, these horses may have been in the auction circuit for some time, being exposed to every communicable disease around. It is not uncommon for horses to develop colds, influenza, or even strangles after being run through an auction.

If you have other horses at home, any horse you bring home from an auction needs to be quarantined for two to four weeks to allow any incubating illnesses to become apparent. (Quarantining a new horse is *always* good practice, but it is especially crucial for horses coming from auction or from an unknown origin.) While in quarantine, the horse should not be able to touch noses with any other horses, and you should change your clothes and boots and wash your hands well after handling the new horse to prevent the spread of infection. If your home barn is not set up for quarantine, you will need to board the new horse at a facility that offers this service.

Keep in mind, as well, that many horses end up at auctions because their owners have been unable to sell them by other means. They may be chronically lame, aggressive, or dangerous under saddle. There is always the chance that an auction purchase will turn out to be the horse of your dreams, but you must be prepared for the possibility that you may be saddling yourself with an unsuitable horse. If your budget and lifestyle can absorb the potential cost of a large pasture pet, then go ahead and check out your local auction—you may be able to save a life. If you're shopping for your once-in-a-lifetime horse, however, you are better off choosing a safer route, such as horse shopping with a trainer or working with a reputable rescue organization.

Signs of a Good Rescue

It is extremely important to work with a reputable rescue. There are many scams out there, and many people who call themselves "rescues" but are really no different than horse traders who buy and sell horses at auction with little regard for the horse's welfare or the satisfaction of human clients. Consider the following factors when looking for a good rescue to support:

- The rescue has current 501(c)(3) status in good standing.
- The rescue requires applications and conducts site checks for potential adopters.
- The rescue requires adopters to sign adoption contracts.
- The rescue can provide positive recommendations from adopters, veterinarians, and other service providers.
- Horses at the rescue appear happy and healthy, and the facilities are in good condition with no signs of overcrowding.
- Check GuideStar.org to review the rescue's tax return, revealing how much money the rescue has taken in and how it was spent.

Adopting from a Rescue

Horse rescue groups take on the difficult and heart-wrenching, but necessary and rewarding, task of caring for horses that have fallen on hard times. Many rescues take in state seizures—horses that have been taken from their owners by the state due to neglectful care or abusive treatment. They may also acquire horses on their own, by buying them back from kill buyers at auctions, by owners surrendering horses that they can no longer care for, or other means. They rehabilitate these horses as needed, and may try them out under saddle and provide training if appropriate. Horses that are sound and rideable are then offered for adoption. A good rescue will have an application process for potential adopters and will visit your farm and check your references to make sure you will be a suitable owner. They will also have an adoption contract specifying the conditions for adoption. For example, most rescues specify that you cannot sell or breed the horse. If you can no longer keep the horse yourself, you must surrender it back to the rescue.

The good news is that rescues do the hard work of rehabilitation and assessment for you. They will work closely with you to ensure that the horse you adopt is appropriate for your skill level and desired riding discipline. If the horse doesn't work out for you, they will take it back or help you find a new, suitable home for it. Their main interest is the horse's welfare. Adoption fees are typically low (compared with the cost of purchasing outright), and you are assured that any immediate veterinary needs have been handled.

Horse Care

8. What All Horses Need

Food and Water

OF COURSE, THE two basic needs of any living thing are water and food. The water part is simple. Provide your horses with access to clean, fresh water at all times. Period. Scrub and refill stall water buckets daily, and check them often throughout the day to make sure they're full. If a stalled horse empties his bucket overnight, provide him with two buckets. For pastured horses, check the trough several times a day and scrub it each time it needs filling (possibly only every two or three days, depending on the size of the trough and number of horses using it). A splash of bleach (followed by a clean-water rinse) will help prevent the growth of algae between scrubbings. In winter, use heated buckets or trough de-icers to keep the water not only ice-free, but pleasantly drinkable. Horses don't like to drink ice-cold water, so they may not drink enough if it's not warmed slightly. Most such heaters are equipped with thermometers that turn them on in freezing temperatures and off when it warms up, so they're simple and labor-free to use.

Food for horses is a much more complex issue. I cover nutrition and feeding in greater depth in chapter 9, but the basics of the issues are as follows:

- Hay or pasture should be the basis of every horse's diet.
- Assess the need for grain or other additives on an individual basis for each horse.

- Always feed the best quality hay and grain. Cheap, poor-quality feed is unhealthy and will cost you more in the long run by having to feed more of it.
- Hay or pasture alone may not provide sufficient nutrients. Add vitamin/mineral supplements as needed.

Every horse's nutritional needs are different, so I can't give you a specific diet to follow for all of your horses. Read chapter 9, as well as any of the excellent books available on the subject of equine nutrition, do research online and in magazines, and arm yourself with as much knowledge as possible. This way you can tailor your feeding program to each horse's unique needs.

Horse Chores

Daily

Feed (at least twice a day)

Visual inspection of each horse

Administer medications as needed

Clean stalls, run-in sheds, and paddocks

Sweep aisle and tidy barn

Check water and empty, scrub, refill as needed; drain and roll up hose

Turn in/turn out

Groom and pick hooves as needed

Blanket changes

Fly spray, take off/put on fly masks and sheets

Weekly

Rotate pastures

Bleach and scrub water troughs

Re-bed stalls as needed

Clean tack

Feed store run for grain, shavings, etc.

Put out new round bale (if using)

Monthly or bimonthly

Mow pastures

Clean out paddock with tractor

Check and repair fencing as needed

Weed-whack fence lines

Deworm horses as needed

Farrier or trimmer appointments

Buy and put up hay (if storage space is limited)

Purchase supplements

Bathe horses as needed

Check and replace salt/mineral blocks

Turn composting manure piles

Annual or semiannual

Fertilize and re-seed pastures

Add and grade footing in paddocks and run-in sheds

Spread manure on pastures

Build new fences as needed

Build new stalls or shelters as needed

Buy and put up hay (if you have enough storage space for the year)

Install/remove heated water buckets and trough de-icers

Dental appointments

Vet appointments for vaccinations and wellness exams

Example Daily Routines

Work at Home

7 AM Bring horses in (if needed) and feed grain and 1 flake hay each. While they're eating, clean shed and check water; dump, scrub, and start filling water if needed.

7:30 AM Turn horses back out and feed 1 flake hay each in pasture. Turn off water and roll up hose.

7:45 AM Back in house to wake kids and get them ready for day care or school.

8:45 AM to 1 PM Work.

1 PM Feed lunch hay—1 flake each in pasture. Lunch break for me.

1:30 PM to 3 PM Work.

3 PM Groom and tack up.

3:15 PM Ride.

4:15 PM Untack, hose horse if needed, return horse to pasture, tidy barn, and sweep aisle.

4:45 PM Leave to pick up child from day care.

5:30 PM Bring horses in (if needed) and feed grain.

5:45 PM Turn horses back out and feed 2 flakes hay each.

10 PM Night check. Feed 2 flakes hay each.

Work Outside the Home

5 AM Bring horses in (if needed) and feed grain and 1 flake hay each. While they're eating, groom and tack up one horse.

5:15 AM Turn horses back out (except riding horse).

5:20 AM Ride.

6:20 AM Untack, hose horse if needed, return horse to pasture, tidy barn, and sweep aisle. Feed 2 flakes hay each in pasture.

6:45 AM Back in house to get ready for work, wake kids, and get them ready for day care or school.

7:45 AM Bring kids to school or day care.

8:30 AM to 5 PM Work.

5:15 PM Pick up kids.

5:30 PM Bring horses in (if needed) and feed grain. While they're eating, clean shed and check water; dump, scrub, and start filling water if needed.

5:45 PM Turn horses back out and feed 2 flakes hay each.

10 PM Night check. Feed 2 flakes hay each.

Companionship

The rare horse can exist happily in a vacuum of companionship. There are horses out there who live solitary lives, in a pasture alone, befriended only by their owners, and they may seem to do just fine. However, the vast majority of horses are extremely unhappy when

FIRST: Horses are most content when they have companions.
MIDDLE: Companion animals don't technically have to be equines...
LAST: Horses need the freedom to kick up their heels.

living alone. Horses evolved as herd animals, and are most content and fulfilled when living in a herd. A solitary horse is ever on alert against danger, never able to let a herdmate take over guard duty so he can relax fully. Horses in a group spend much of their day socializing, grooming each other, and having discussions about the pecking order; a lone horse is denied these social outlets. Thus, a solitary horse may become stressed, anxious, and bored.

It's ideal to keep at least two horses (although most horses are even happier in a larger group). If you plan to keep only one riding horse, consider finding a companion horse to keep him company. Older horses or those that are pasture-sound but unsuitable for riding are often free or cheap to acquire. To keep costs down, look for an easy keeper, even a pony or a mini (although you may have to closely monitor their grass intake to prevent obesity or laminitis). A donkey can also be an excellent companion with low maintenance costs. They are quite noisy and serve as an excellent guard animal to protect any livestock or poultry you may have. If you prefer not to have another equine, a few goats can serve as an admirable substitute. Goats come with their own set of management requirements and problems, though, so to me it seems best to stick to one species.

Turnout and Exercise

All horses need freedom to wander and stretch their legs and minds daily. Some types of show horses are kept in stalls at all times except during training, but to me this is not an ideal way of keeping horses. It's neither good for their minds and bodies nor efficient for the home horsekeeper. In my opinion, the best way to keep horses on a small scale is 24/7 turnout. It's cost- and labor-effective, and it keeps the horses happy and healthy. Even if you decide to stall your horses for part of the day, be sure to turn them out for at least twelve hours every day.

Shelter

Horses that live outdoors need access to a sturdy, wind-resistant, three-sided roofed shelter to seek protection from wind, rain, snow, sun, and insects. Most states have requirements for this type of shelter. If you have a barn with a stall for each horse, and you're vigilant about bringing the horses inside in adverse conditions, you can get away without having a run-in shed, but it's really easiest to have one that the horses can choose to use at will. Read more about shelters, barns, and stalls in chapter 2.

Grooming

Okay, so horses don't *need* grooming if they aren't being ridden; they certainly won't die without it. But grooming is an important part of keeping your horses happy, healthy, and beautiful. Regular grooming sessions afford you the opportunity to carefully check over the horse for any injuries, cuts, swellings, skin conditions, hoof problems, and attitude changes that can signal a health problem. They are also a chance to bond with your horse, get to know him better, and

ABOVE: My horses have access to their shelter at all times.

maintain his training for routine handling. Grooming is a source of joy for most horse lovers and horses alike, which is reason enough to do it. Each time you ride, drive, or work your horse, you do need to groom him before and after to make sure his skin and coat are clean under his tack and to make sure there are no foreign objects in his hooves. See chapter 10 for more on the subject.

Training

Yes, *all* horses need training. Even horses that are not being ridden need training on their ground manners and handling. Each time you handle your horse, you are training him, whether consciously or not. If you're grooming your horse and he pins his ears and threatens to kick you, and you back off, what have you just taught him? You've

Costs of Horsekeeping

My claim is that keeping a horse can cost less than $100 per month (depending on costs of feed and bedding in your area of the country), and here I intend to prove it. Below is a chart listing all of the monthly and annual expenses for maintaining a horse, broken down by month. Daily expenses such as feed have been calculated by multiplying the amount of feed per day by 30 days (for example, 6 pounds of grain per day, times 30 days per month, divided by 50 pounds per bag of grain, times $18 per bag of grain, equals $64.8, or approximately $65, per month). Annual and bimonthly expenses have been calculated by determining the total per year and dividing by 12 to get a monthly average (for example, 6 shoeings per year multiplied by $100 per shoeing, divided by 12 months per year, equals $50 per month).

The Maximum column lists costs for the most expensive type of horse. It assumes a horse being fed one bale of hay (at $4.25 per bale), 0.5 pounds of vitamin/mineral supplement (at $20 per 50-pound bag), and 6 pounds of grain (at $18 for a 50-pound bag) per day; living part-time in a stall that needs 3 bags of shav-

MONTHLY EXPENSES FOR ONE HORSE

	Maximum	Minimum
Hay	$150	$0
Vit/min supp	$6	$6
Grain	$65	$0
Bedding	$60	$0
Deworm	$45.50	$34
Supplements	$50	$0
Hoof care	$50	$36
Dental care	$10	$5
Routine vet	$17	$17
Total	$393.50	$98

ings per week at $5 per bag; on a rotation deworming schedule (an average of $7 every 8 weeks); being given supplements totaling about $50 per month; with shoes ($100 every 8 weeks); dental care every six months ($60 every six months); and an average of $200 in annual routine vet care (vaccinations and exam).

The Minimum column lists costs for the least expensive type of horse. It assumes a horse being fed no hay (i.e., pasture is sufficient; of course, in winter you'll have to feed hay no matter what, so this number is really only valid in summer), 0.5 pounds of vitamin/mineral supplement (at $20 per 50-pound bag), and no grain; living outdoors with shelter (no bedding); on a targeted deworming schedule ($20 for annual fecal exam plus 2 dewormings at an average of $7 each); no supplements; with barefoot trims ($50 every 6 weeks); and annual dental care ($60 every 12 months). So following my suggestions for horse care (depending, of course, on your local costs for hay, grain, bedding, and services, which can vary greatly), a single horse can cost you as much as $394 per month or as little as $98 per month, including all annual expenses. If you only consider daily expenses, that "Minimum" type horse only costs $6 per month!

taught him that he doesn't have to respect you (or anyone else). Next time that threat could become a real kick. The same goes for any situation in which you're handling your horse. He needs to be polite, respectful, and patient when being turned in or out, waiting for his dinner, loading on a trailer, or having farrier or vet work done. These are all training opportunities.

Any rideable horse should have a base level of under-saddle training as well, for his own protection. What I mean is that if something were to happen to you that forced you to sell off your herd, any horse that's not trained for riding has a much greater chance of ending up somewhere unpleasant, such as in a low-end auction ring or on a truck headed for a slaughterhouse in Canada or Mexico. This may

sound dramatic or extreme, but it's true. These days a horse with no training has very little chance of finding a loving home. Have your horses trained, at least to walk, trot, and canter under saddle, to give them the best chance of a happy future.

Vet, Farrier, and Dental Care

All horses need to be seen by a vet annually for routine vaccinations. Most states require horses to have a rabies vaccination, at minimum. Your vet will advise you as to the recommended vaccinations for other communicable diseases that are prevalent in your area. Horses also need regular deworming, about which see more below.

All horses need hoof care, whether they are shod or barefoot. Most shod horses need to be trimmed and re-shod every six to eight weeks, while barefoot horses may need trimming every four to six weeks. Left unattended, horses' hooves will continue to grow, causing discomfort, lameness, hoof damage, and sometimes chronic hoof problems.

Although they are less visible and obvious than the hooves, horses' teeth also grow throughout their lifetimes. They wear down through use, but often wear unevenly, causing sharp points, hooks, and other imperfections that can abrade the cheeks and gums and cause difficulty chewing. Teeth need to be checked and floated (filed down) by an equine dentist annually. See chapter 11 for more details on veterinary care, hoof care, and equine dentistry.

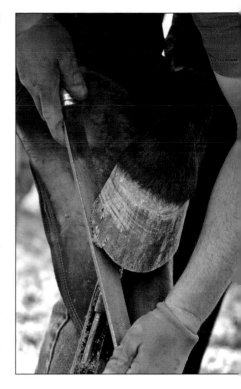

Common Myths About Horse Care

There are many myths that are propagated among the horse community, whether consciously or simply by virtue of the fact that most boarding stables seem to abide by these unspoken "rules" of horse care. In many cases these methods and policies exist for the convenience of the boarding stable's management. That's not to say that a boarding stable's methods are wrong or bad for the horses. On the contrary, there are many "right" ways to keep horses. However, when you move your horses home, you will find that the economics of keeping two or three horses at home are very different from keeping twenty or thirty horses in a boarding stable environment.

For example, in order to preserve their pastures and allow all horses to have daily access to grass, a large boarding stable may need to keep horses in their stalls for most of the day, only allowing them into the pasture for a couple of hours. Letting all the horses roam free would quickly overwhelm and destroy the pastures. The result is that owners who have only ever boarded their horses may believe, because they've never seen another way, that horses need to live in stalls. However, at home, you may be able to let your horses have 24/7 access to the pastures during seasons when the grass is growing. There are many such misunderstandings about horse care. The good news is that the truth often saves you money. Read on.

Myth: All Horses Need Grain.

The truth is that horses evolved to survive on grass and other wild plants. Domesticated horses often lack access to free-choice pasture or hay, and therefore their calorie and nutritional needs must be supplemented with a concentrated, man-made source—grain. If horses have access to free-choice hay or pasture, the majority will keep their weight well and will not need *any grain at all*. In fact, feeding large quantities of grain can be unhealthy for horses, contributing to gastric ulcers, colic, laminitis and founder, insulin resistance, and many other common equine maladies.

Because hay is expensive and good-quality pastures of adequate size are hard to come by in most areas, boarding stables usually compensate for the lack of forage by feeding grain. When you keep your horses at home, you have the luxury of feeding them as much top-quality hay as they need to maintain their weight. Every horse has a unique metabolism. Some are hard keepers, and will need free-choice hay. Others are "air ferns" and need only a few flakes of hay per day. Watch your horses carefully, and stay alert to signs that they need less or more hay. (See Body Condition Score on page 167.)

It is important to seek out the best quality hay that you can find. The best hay will have a higher percentage of the nutrients that horses need, and will also contain more protein and calories. It is actually a false economy to buy cheap, low-quality hay, since you will inevitably have to feed more of it. Last year, due to the six weeks of rain during hay harvesting season, it was nearly impossible to find good hay. I had to make do with what was available, and the result was that my horses each went through a bale of hay a day in the winter. This year, I've located a source of excellent hay, and I've found that I have to cut back significantly to prevent them from getting fat. Although the price per bale is higher, I am actually saving money by being able to feed less hay. Read more about hay on page 173.

There are, of course, exceptions. Some horses may need more nutrients and calories than hay alone can provide. Horses that may need grain include: nursing or pregnant mares; growing youngsters; horses in hard work; older horses whose worn-down teeth may not allow them to chew hay efficiently; hard keepers whose metabolism is naturally higher; horses that are ill or recovering from an illness; horses in a rescue situation whose weight needs to be brought up from well below normal. If you do find that you need to provide grain to your horse, be sure to choose a good-quality product. Talk to feed reps, talk to your vet, and talk to other owners in the area. Do not buy the cheapest grain you can find. Like hay, buying cheap grain is a false economy. You will have to feed more to achieve the desired results, and you will be filling your horse with unhealthy sugars and fillers. Read more about choosing a good grain on page 176.

In some cases, your grass or hay may be lower quality and may need to be supplemented with a vitamin/mineral supplement or ration balancer that provides the missing nutrients. Clear signs that your forage may lack nutrients are dull coats, brittle hooves, and weight loss. There are several products available that meet this need. Ask your feed store to recommend a good vitamin/mineral mix to balance out your hay's nutritional profile. I feed my horses Blue Seal's Min-a-Vite Lite. This is a pelleted grain-like product that contains concentrated amounts of necessary nutrients without the bulk and high calories of grain. I feed two cups a day and don't have to worry that my horses aren't getting what they need. In addition, the soil in some geographic locations is deficient in selenium, a necessary micronutrient. If you live in such a region, you'll need to add a vitamin E and selenium supplement to all of your horses.

Horses Have to Live in Stalls

No, they do not. Most horses, in fact, are much happier living outdoors. They can quickly become bored and pent-up when they are kept in stalls for much of the day. Think about it—even if you turn your horse out all day, he is still in his stall at night for up to twelve hours. Twelve hours locked in a box! Many boarding stables offer even less turnout, with horses staying in their stalls for up to twenty-three hours of every day. Psychologically and physiologically, this is unhealthy for a horse. Horses evolved to move constantly, roaming throughout the day in search of forage. They can quickly become anxious and stressed when confined. They are herd animals who are only satisfied when they can interact naturally with a group of other members of their own kind. Their lymphatic systems require the concussion of movement to function properly; this is why some horses become "stocked up" when in a stall for a period of time—their lymphatic fluids literally pool in the lower legs, causing swelling. A horse that is eating hay in a stall stands still for hours at a time. A horse grazing in a pasture walks almost constantly in search of that next blade of grass. This continuous, low-level movement helps maintain muscle tone, encourages circulation to the lower limbs and hooves, burns off excess energy, and improves digestive function. In addition, the pastured horse has the opportunity to gallop, buck, frolic, and play whenever the urge strikes.

You may find that many behavioral problems simply evaporate when your horse moves to an outdoor living situation. Cribbing, weaving, pacing, and stall-walking are all anxiety-caused vices that can be virtually cured by 24/7 turnout. Bucking, jigging, spooking, bolting, and other under-saddle behavior issues are often caused or exacerbated by excess energy. More turnout allows the horse to exercise at will, so he will be calmer and less likely to act up while being ridden. The same goes for horses that are difficult and reactive while being handled.

The ideal situation for most horses is to live outdoors in a group in a large paddock or pasture with access to a shelter, such as a three-sided run-in shed. The good news for you is that it is much less time-consuming and expensive to maintain horses in this kind of set-up. Stalled horses need to be turned out and brought in daily. Their stalls need to be thoroughly cleaned and re-bedded at least once a day, if not more. They will go through three or four bags of shavings a week, at $5 a pop. Water buckets need to be dumped, scrubbed, and filled each day, and probably filled at least two or three more times throughout the day. In contrast, horses who live outside are much more self-sufficient. Because they can come and go from their shelter, it will stay much cleaner. Some owners don't even use bedding in the shelter. I do bed mine with shavings, because I like to know that there's a clean, dry, soft place for the horses to stand or lie down if they so choose. Even so, I have only one shed to clean each day instead of four stalls. I go through one or two bags of shavings per week for all four horses, instead of the eight to sixteen bags I would use if they were all stalled. That alone is a huge savings. I have a large, seventy-gallon trough that I dump, scrub, and refill approximately every three days, saving me lots of time in daily chores.

Another factor to consider is the fact that occasionally, despite your best intentions, you may not be able to get to your chores in a timely manner. On New Year's Day, you may want to sleep in an extra hour or two. Or perhaps there is an emergency that needs to be handled at work and you can't get home until 9 PM. Any number of unexpected circumstances can arise, preventing you from getting home. Your mind will be at ease knowing your horses are outside with access to grass and plenty of water in their trough, rather than trapped in filthy stalls for hours with no hay and no water.

Now, there are many times when a stall can be a good and useful tool in your horsekeeping toolbox. Although my horses live outdoors with a shed, I do have stalls and I bring the horses in for many reasons. A horse may need stall rest because of an injury. We like to have them all in and handy for a vet or farrier's visit. There may be one horse whose feeding needs are very different, so he has to be separated at meal times. We use the stalls for grooming, tacking up, and untacking. We put the retired horse in her stall while we ride the other two so that she can't run around and injure herself if she gets upset about being alone. We bring all the horses in when the weather is extremely bad—either unbearably hot and buggy in the summer or unbearably cold, snowy, and windy in the winter.

Many home-based horse owners never bring their horses into stalls due to weather at all. They stay out, with shelter available, no matter the weather. Personally, during those frigid January nor'easters when the temperature drops below zero, the snow is flying, and the wind is whipping past my bedroom window like a banshee, I sleep much easier knowing my horses are tucked into their stalls, safe and comfortable. Sure, they won't die being left out. But is that really the minimum standard of care you want to provide for your animals—that they won't die? Better to know that they are not suffering from the cold. The ideal scenario is to have a stall available for every horse, even if you don't use the stalls every day.

Breeding

Breeding horses may seem, at first glance, like a great way to earn money. However, except for large operations with top-quality stallions and carefully selected broodmares, breeding is generally a losing proposition. I strongly discourage any beginning horse owner from breeding at all, let alone breeding with the intention of earning a profit. Breeding horses requires a great deal of hard-earned experience and expertise, and involves great risk both in terms of potential money lost and the risks to the health of the mare and foal.

In order to breed horses successfully, you need to start with the best quality mare that you can—a registered mare with a blue-blooded pedigree, ideal conformation for her breed and discipline, a pleasant temperament, ideally a proven record in the show ring, and a history of successful breedings. Next you need to locate the perfect match for this mare—a stallion with equally stellar pedigree, conformation, temperament, and performance history. The stud fee for such a stallion will not be inexpensive—depending on his breed, it could be several thousand dollars.

On top of the stud fee, take into consideration the costs of maintaining and caring for the mare throughout conception and pregnancy (she will need increased top-quality food to eat as she gestates and nurses her baby); veterinary costs associated with breeding, including a breeding soundness exam for the mare, insemination, pregnancy checks, and extra vaccinations; veterinary costs associated with the delivery of the foal; and care, feeding, and training of the foal as it grows. Even after all of that, there is always a risk that the foal will be sick, injured, or may not even survive. You can see that all of these costs will quickly escalate into the thousands of dollars. In order to recoup your costs, let alone turn a profit, you'll have to be able to sell the foal for quite a high price. As you're no doubt aware, horses these days are not selling for much, especially not young, unstarted babies. Poorly bred, poorly conformed, unregistered young horses—even weanlings—often end up at auctions, where they sell for meat price and earn a one-way ticket to Canada or Mexico. Not that you, as a caring owner, would send your foal to an auction, but this gives you an idea of the market value of that sort of animal.

If I haven't scared you off and you're still interested in breeding, please do some research into the subject and discuss it thoroughly with your veterinarian and experienced horse breeders in your area. Make sure you know the costs and risks, and what you're getting yourself into, before you start. Armed with all of the knowledge and community support you can muster, follow the horseman's wisdom: Breed the best to the best, and hope for the best.

All Horses Need to Wear Shoes

There are many good reasons for horses to wear shoes. The main ones are that they protect the hoof walls from chipping and cracking, and they protect the soles from bruising and soreness. What some owners don't realize, however, is that a healthy hoof with a good barefoot trim can serve these functions on its own. Provided the horse has the underlying genetics and good nutrition, and that he is being maintained on a regular basis by a trimmer skilled in barefoot trimming, he can grow a hard, solid hoof wall that will resist chips and cracks. His sole will become calloused and thick, protecting the sensitive inner parts of the hoof from contact with the ground. For horses that are in transition from being shod to barefoot, or for horses that are ridden over rocky or hard surfaces, hoof boots can offer additional protection.

Shoes themselves can also be problematic. A horse that pulls off a shoe can do considerable damage to the hoof wall. A shoe holds in snow and ice in winter, leading to a buildup on the sole of the hoof until the horse is literally walking on balls of ice, a dangerous and unpleasant condition for the horse and a difficult task for the human who must chip it out. Similarly, a shoe can hold in dirt, manure, and mud, allowing it to pack deeply into the clefts of the frog and contributing to hoof infections like thrush. An unshod hoof allows dirt to fall out more easily as the horse moves. Some barefoot enthusiasts argue that a shoe prevents the horse's hoof from performing one of its most important functions, shock absorption, by eliminating its ability to expand and contract naturally. In a group turnout situation, shoes can be dangerous; a kick from a shod hoof does much more damage than an unshod one.

More good news for the owner of a barefoot horse: It's less expensive! A barefoot horse may need to be trimmed slightly more frequently (every four to six weeks) than a shod horse (every six to eight weeks), but each trim costs significantly less than a trim and shoeing for a shod horse.

Now, this is not to say that all shoes are bad and that all horses are better off without them. Some horses simply do not have the genetic makeup to grow strong hoof walls. Some have flat or thin soles, making them vulnerable to hoof soreness or bruising. Every horse is unique, and should be evaluated on an individual basis. Talk to your vet and farrier about whether your horse may be able to live and work comfortably and safely without shoes. Horses who are not being worked generally do not need shoes at all. The ideal candidate to go barefoot is a horse who has naturally strong walls and thick soles, and is worked on surfaces that approximate the surface he lives on. That is, a horse cannot be expected to go from a soft, grassy pasture to a rocky, root-covered trail without some discomfort. His hooves simply are not acclimated to it. But a horse who lives in a gravel-covered paddock and who works in a sand arena should be just fine.

Horses Must Be Fed on a Strict Schedule

Many people believe that horses need to be fed at the exact same time every day, or else they will colic, become stressed, or suffer some other terrible fate. It does seem to be the case that horses can "tell time," and if they are accustomed to being fed at, say, 5:30 every evening, they will commence hysterics at promptly 5:31 if they have not been fed. The remedy for this is not, as many assume, to feed on a strict schedule to avoid equine stress, but rather the opposite. If you feed your horses according to a very loose time clock—say, breakfast at any time between 6 AM and 9 AM and dinner at any time between 4 PM and 7 PM—they will not come to anticipate their precise dinnertime, so anxiety and stress are vastly reduced if you're "late" with their meal one day. This works especially well if you're only doling out grain at those times, and they have free access to hay or pasture, so they're never actually hungry. Not maintaining a strict schedule has benefits to your personal life as well as reducing equine stress around feeding times. You can sleep in a little on Sunday, for example, or run a few errands after work, knowing that the horses are fine waiting a bit for their meals, and are not pacing the fence line in a frantic state wondering when you will appear.

Horses Have to Be Dewormed Every Six Weeks

For decades, the recommended practice was to deworm all horses every six weeks, rotating through a variety of dewormers designed to kill a broad spectrum of internal parasites. Current research is changing that trend. Many vets now recommend an annual fecal egg count to determine which specific parasites are infecting each horse, and deworming specifically to combat those worms. The concern is that rotation deworming may be creating a new generation of evolved superparasites that are immune to the standard dewormers, much like how overuse of antibiotics in human medicine has led to the creation of drug-resistant superbacteria.

Dr. David Jefferson of Maine Equine Associates explains the thinking behind this new style of deworming:

> Most horses are able to co-exist with parasites. It has proven to be unrealistic to make our animals parasite-free. So all horses carry some worms, but seem to have their own resistance to them. . . . However, there are some horses that don't. Parasites in those horses thrive. . . . The horses that carry this big burden of parasites are called "shedders," and are largely responsible for contaminating the ground with worm eggs. . . . It is the shedder horses that revised worming programs are targeting.
>
> You can't tell by looking which of your horses is a shedder. It could be the healthiest looking horse in the herd. Fecal exams have to be done on all of your horses to determine who are the shedders. The exams are performed either by veterinarians in their office or they might send the sample to a commercial lab. Shedders are identified by a very large number of eggs per gram of manure. Once identified, the shedders are the ones who get the intensive deworming attention, while others in the barn may need only once or twice a year worming. This system is called targeted worming. It is a program best guided by your veterinarian.
>
> The object of targeted worming is to cut way back on the amount of worm medicine being used and so lessen the ability of parasites to develop immunity to it. . . . At the moment there are no new wormers being developed, so resistance will become more and more of a problem. (*The Horse's Maine*, May 2011)

Yet again, making this horsekeeping change can end up saving the horse owner money in the long run. While the cost of having your vet perform an annual fecal count on each horse may seem like a high one-time expense, you will save the cost of buying dewormer every six weeks. Discuss this option with your vet to determine if targeted deworming is the right choice for your horses.

Horses on Pasture Don't Need Anything Else to Eat

Some easy keepers may be just fine on an all-grass diet, provided the pasture is well maintained and rotated, with a healthy mixture of horse-appropriate grasses. Unfortunately, many pastures are not equipped to meet the nutritional needs of horses, or they may be overgrazed. Tradition states that one horse needs one acre of grass, but that's only valid in an environment where growing conditions are good. In an arid environment where the grass is poorer and grows more slowly, each horse may need several acres to browse. Most small-scale horse owners simply don't have access to enough good-quality pasture. To offset any nutritional deficiencies in your grass, add a vitamin/mineral supplement to each horse's daily ration. If a particular horse can't maintain a healthy weight on pasture alone, consider adding a high-quality grain or a fibrous nutrient source such as beet pulp, alfalfa cubes or pellets, or simply extra hay fed in addition to pasture grazing.

Horses Are Extremely Expensive

Well, okay, this one is true. Horses certainly are a luxury pet that most Americans simply can't afford. But there is a wide variety of horsekeeping styles that can make horses relatively affordable or place them within the realm of the super-rich. You can keep your six-figure warmblood in full training at a high-end dressage or hunter facility in the suburbs at a cost of several thousand dollars per month. Or you can keep your $500 off-the-track Thoroughbred at home in a rural area for less than a hundred dollars a month. It's true! Less than a hundred dollars a month! It will take planning, know-how, and some sacrifices (you didn't really need that trendy new pair of breeches anyway, right?), but it is possible.

Consider the fact that most middle-class Americans have some sort of expensive recreational hobby. They may be into motorcycles, golf, biking, skiing, snowmobiling, classic cars or racecars, or any number of other pursuits. Owning horses is like many of these hobbies, with one important caveat: The horse is a living being. If a golfing enthusiast loses his job, he can simply cancel his club membership and stop paying greens fees until he gets back on his feet. A horse owner can't simply stop feeding her horse. Yes, in a worst-case scenario the horses can be sold, but in the current economic climate, it is hard to sell even a high-quality horse. One that is old, unsound, or poorly trained may be impossible even to give away. So keep this point in mind as you decide to delve into the world of horse ownership. It doesn't have to be crazy expensive—and I'll give you pointers along the way on how to save money—but it is a commitment. It's not just a hobby; it's a lifestyle.

9. Feeding and Nutrition

EQUINE NUTRITION IS a topic worthy of years of study; indeed, it's possible to get a university degree on the subject. Entire books have been devoted to it, so here I'll just give an overview of some of the important points to remember.

Body Condition Score

There's much more to the concept of equine nutrition than just weight gain or loss, but body condition can give us a quick visual glimpse of whether things are on the right track, or not, for a given horse. The Henneke Body Condition Score (BCS) assigns a numerical value to a horse's condition, from 1 being near death from starvation to 9 being severely obese. There is no set ideal number for all horses, as the ideal body condition varies by body type, breed, and even discipline. An eventer or endurance horse, for example, should fall in the range of 4 to 5, while a Quarter Horse or dressage horse looks his best in the 5 to 7 range. For most pleasure horses, a BCS of 5 or 6 is about right.

All horse owners should be familiar with the concept of body condition score in order to objectively monitor their horses' condition. It's easy to look at your own horse each day and think he looks just great, when in reality he's dangerously obese or underweight. "Barn blindness" refers to the rose-colored glasses we tend to don when looking at our own beloved equines, such that we think they are the most beautiful creatures on the planet, when in reality they may have glaring conformational defects or, in this case, poor condition. The body condition score allows us to replace these rose-colored lenses with 20/20 vision. How does your horse rate?

The BCS takes into account six specific anatomical landmarks: the loin, ribs, tailhead, withers, neck, and shoulders. The specific descriptions for each numerical score are offered below.

BCS 1: Emaciated. Bony structures of neck, shoulders, and withers easily noticeable. Spinous processes, along the ribs, topline, point of hip, and point of buttock all project prominently, with an obvious ridge down the back. Individual vertebrae may be identifiable. The animal is extremely emaciated; no fatty tissue can be felt.

BCS 2: Very Thin. Bony structures of the neck, shoulders and withers are faintly discernible. Spinous processes, ribs, topline, point of hip, and buttock are prominent. Animal is emaciated.

BCS 3: Thin. Neck, withers, and shoulder are accentuated, but not obviously thin. Tailhead is prominent. Slight fat cover over ribs, but still easily discernible. Spinous processes, point of hip, and point of buttock are rounded, but easily discernible.

BCS 4: Moderately Thin: Neck, withers, and shoulders are not obviously thin. Ribs are faintly discernible. Point of hips and buttocks are not visually discernible. Fat can be felt around the tailhead,

prominence somewhat dependent upon conformation. There is a slight negative crease (a ridge) along the topline, especially over the loins and hindquarters.

BCS 5: Moderate. Neck, withers, and shoulder appear rounded and blend smoothly into the body. Ribs cannot be seen but are easily felt. Back is level with neither a ridge nor a gully along the topline. Fat around tailhead is beginning to feel spongey.

BCS 6: Moderately Fleshy. Fat beginning to be deposited along the neck, withers, and shoulders. Fat over the ribs beginning to feel spongey; ribs cannot easily be felt. Fat around tailhead feels soft. May be slight positive crease (gully) along the topline.

BCS 7: Fleshy. Fat deposited along neck and withers and behind shoulder. Individual ribs can be felt, but with noticeable filling between ribs. Slight positive crease down back. Fat around tailhead feels soft.

BCS 8: Obese. Noticeable thickening of neck. Area along withers is filled with fat, area behind shoulder is filled in flush with body. Ribs cannot be felt, noticeable positive crease down back, fat around tailhead is very soft.

BCS 9: Extremely Obese. Bulging fat along neck, shoulders, and withers. Flank is filled in flush. Patchy fat appearing over ribs; obvious positive crease down back.

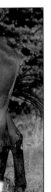

FIRST: This horse is about a BCS 7 or 8—definitely overweight.

MIDDLE: With her prominent spine, rib, and hip bones, this horse ranks about a BCS 2 or 3—much too thin. Her protruding belly may be deceiving, but considering her overall condition, the belly is most likely a result of worms, too much low-quality hay, or even pregnancy.

LAST: Under her fuzzy winter coat, this horse is in good condition—about a BCS 5 or 6.

My Horse Is Too Thin

Horses can lose weight for a variety of reasons—stress, intestinal parasites, gastric ulcers, increased exercise, dental problems, illness, or simply, and most commonly, lack of adequate calories in the diet. After ruling out all other problems, especially teeth and worms, it's time to start bulking up the horse's diet. The simplest way to accomplish this is just to add more hay. In consultation with your vet, determine the horse's ideal weight, and feed good-quality hay at a rate of 2 percent of the ideal body weight per day. Many hard-keeping horses can be fed free-choice hay at all times with no ill consequences. If you can't find good enough hay or if even free-choice hay just isn't cutting it, there are several options.

Grain. In general, it isn't the greatest idea to simply feed loads of grain to try to increase weight. Grain concentrates can be hard on a horse's sensitive digestive system, and excessive amounts of simple carbohydrates (sugars) found in grain can cause health and behavior problems. It's best not to feed more than 5 pounds of grain at a single meal. If your horse seems to need more than 10 pounds of grain per day, add a third meal separated from breakfast and dinner by at least 4 hours. As always, feed the best-quality feed that you can buy. For a hard keeper, make sure the fat content is high—10 to 12 percent is best.

Beet pulp. Beet pulp is a by-product of the sugar beet industry often used in animal feeds. It's an excellent source of fiber and calories in the equine diet, filling a nutritional role similar to hay or grass as opposed to grain or other concentrates. Unlike grain, it can be safely fed in large quantities. It's also extremely inexpensive; at my feed store, a 50-pound bag only costs about $10. You can buy it in pelleted or shredded dehydrated forms. Personally I prefer the pellets, as I find them easier to handle and measure, but this is a matter of personal preference. In any case, make sure your beet pulp doesn't contain added molasses, as this increases unwanted and unnecessary sugars in the diet.

Beet pulp must be soaked in plenty of water for at least two hours (for pellets; shreds may only take 15 minutes or so to soak) before being fed. Opinions differ on whether it's true that dry beet pulp can cause choke or impaction colic by drawing water out of the digestive tract, but to me it isn't worth the risk. Plus, soaking makes beet pulp much more palatable, increases its apparent volume, and allows it to serve as a nice moist vehicle for powdery medications or supplements. Start with 2 cups or so (measured dry; if using pellets, this should soak up to about a quart) fed twice a day, and increase gradually until you start seeing a noticeable change in the horse's weight.

Rice bran. This granular or pelleted product contains more than 20 percent fat, so it's an excellent concentrated source of calories. Add 1 cup to each meal to easily add fat to the diet. One drawback of rice bran is that it's high in omega-6 fatty acids, which can increase inflammation. The omega-6s can be balanced by adding a source of omega-3 fatty acids to the diet, such as flax seed or fresh green grass. I have always thought a meal of beet pulp mash topped with rice bran seemed like a delicious meal for a hard keeper. The horses seem to agree.

Alfalfa cubes, hay pellets, or chopped bagged forage. These processed forms of hay can be helpful in a situation where high-quality hay is unavailable, the horse can't eat normal hay due to dental or respiratory problems, or the owner wants to be able to add a hay source that the horse can eat quickly at meal times, without having to share with other horses in a turnout group. Alfalfa cubes are a good choice for horses that may need additional protein in the diet, and the additional calcium in alfalfa is beneficial for horses with ulcers. Alfalfa cubes can be soaked like beet pulp to create a pleasant, palatable mash. Keep in mind that some horses seem to become more high-strung when being fed alfalfa. Chopped bagged forage can be a useful option, especially when local hay quality is low or the horse can't eat hay, but it is expensive, often contains added molasses or other fillers, and may be susceptible to botulism contamination.

Oils. One common way to add fat and calories to a horse's diet is to top-dress his meal with a cup of oil. This is certainly a concentrated way to add fat, since oil is 100 percent fat. Personally, I'm not a big fan of adding oil. It's messy, for one. And the less expensive forms of oil, such as corn oil and vegetable oil, tend to be very high in inflammatory omega-6s. Better quality oils, like flaxseed oil, are high in beneficial omega-3s, but are quite pricy. Fish oil is also high in omega-3s, but I hesitate to add any kind of animal product to the diet of an herbivore that evolved to eat grass, not fish.

My Horse Is Too Fat

Obesity is a dangerous condition for a horse. Most experienced horsepeople would say it's better for a horse to be a little too thin than a little too fat. Obesity predisposes a horse to a host of devastating conditions, such as laminitis and founder, insulin resistance, colic, and other digestive upsets. Indications of obesity are a cresty neck, a crease down the spine with fat on either side, fat pads around the tail head, and ribs covered so thickly by fat that it's difficult to feel them when pressing firmly with the fingertips.

It's important to limit such a horse's calorie intake to bring him back to a healthy weight. First and foremost, do not feed any grain at all. (However, to make sure the horse is still getting the essential nutrients he needs, make sure to feed a low-calorie concentrated vitamin/mineral supplement.) If the horse is on pasture, create a dry paddock where you can isolate him from the grass for several hours a day. If feeding hay, weigh it and be sure to feed no more than 2 percent of the horse's *ideal* weight. That is, if your horse weighs 1,200 pounds and the vet recommends that he lose 200, feed him no more than 20 pounds of hay per day—2 percent of 1,000 pounds. Try soaking the hay before feeding it to reduce the amount of sugars it contains.

If the horse is rideable, increase the amount of exercise he gets, gradually so as not to overtax him. Add one or two sessions of lungeing per week, or try to spend a little more time trotting and cantering instead of walking during a ride. Ride for an hour instead of 45 minutes. When you feed him his hay, spread it all around the paddock so he has to work a bit to get to each pile. Alternatively, purchase a "slow feeder" or small-hole hay net that makes it more difficult for the horse to pull out the hay. This increases the time it takes him to eat his limited hay ration, keeping him busy and eating for a longer period of time so you won't feel you need to feed more hay due to boredom or hunger. If it's possible to pasture the horse on a hill, do so, and put the hay at the bottom and water at the top so he has to climb the hill several times a day.

In addition to management changes in diet and exercise, it is wise to have your vet check the horse for obesity-related conditions such as thyroid problems, Cushing's disease, and insulin resistance.

Forage: Pasture and Hay

Forage is the foundation of the horse's diet, and is the horse's natural food source. Many horses do very well on a diet of nothing but hay or grass. To serve as the sole source of nutrition for the horse, pastures must be large enough (one to two acres per horse) and healthy enough to provide adequate forage. See the section on Pasture Management in chapter 3 for more on keeping your grass pastures healthy and lush.

When a horse doesn't have access to grass, hay should be fed at a rate of 2 percent of the horse's body weight per day—so, for a 1,000-pound horse, 20 pounds of hay is ideal. This is just a general guideline—hay intake can be increased in very cold weather, or if the horse is underweight or is a hard keeper, or decreased for an obese horse. For horses that aren't prone to obesity, hay can even be fed free-choice.

There are a few nutrients that grass or hay alone may not provide. In some areas of the country, the native soil is deficient in an essential micronutrient called selenium, which must be fed in a supplement or grain type product. One vital nutrient missing from cured hay, although it is abundantly present in fresh grass, is vitamin E, which allows the horse to absorb selenium and supports nervous system function, among other benefits. One option for the pastured or hay-fed horse is to add a general vitamin/mineral supplement or a ration balancer (see below) as insurance that the horse is getting all the nutrients he needs.

To determine the exact nutritional profile of your hay and to pinpoint any deficiencies, you can have a hay analysis performed.

BELOW: High-quality hay or grass should be the foundation of every horse's diet.

Check with your local agricultural extension service for hay analysis resources. This is beneficial if all of your hay comes from the same source; however, if you use multiple hay suppliers throughout the season, you may be better off just feeding a good ration balancer to ward off any potential deficiencies.

Round Bales

These days, many people are turning to round bales—large bales weighing 500 to 800 pounds that can be left out in the pasture for the horses. Round bales are less expensive than small square bales for the same quantity of hay, and save a lot of work each day since hay doesn't need to be fed by individual flakes throughout the day. Round bales are not a perfect solution, however. Under muggy, damp conditions they can quickly become moldy, and mold is very dangerous for horses, causing respiratory problems and colic. Since they are by definition a form of free-choice feeding, easy keepers can quickly become obese when allowed 24/7 access to a round bale. In addition, although the original cost of the bale may be cheaper than for a comparable quantity of hay in small bales, round bales can lead to a lot of waste as the horses tear apart the bale and spread it around on the ground. When purchasing round bales, it is vitally important to choose the best quality hay you can find. It must have been cured and prepared as well as possible, and stored under cover or wrapped in plastic to preserve nutrients and prevent mold. Many cattle farmers routinely feed round bales that have been left out in the elements, so make sure your hay supplier knows you are feeding horses, not cows.

Hay Feeders

You can feed hay right on the ground if you choose. Eating with their heads down is the most natural and healthy position for a horse. But specially designed hay feeders offer several benefits.

In a sandy environment, it's best not to feed hay directly on the ground, as ingesting sand particles can ultimately lead to sand colic. In a muddy or dirty paddock, hay gets trampled into the muck and wasted—or, worse, the horses may eat it anyway and ingest parasites or mold. Finally, hay fed loose is easy for the horses to gobble up quickly. Then they are left standing around with nothing to eat for hours, until the next feeding. It's best for horses to have something to nibble on continuously, for both digestive and mental health.

Enter the slow feeder. These devices are designed to limit the horse's ability to access the hay quickly, so it takes them a much longer time to eat it. A simple small-hole hay net is an inexpensive version of a slow feeder, but you can also buy larger, sturdier contraptions made for use in paddocks, which can hold a whole bale or even a round bale.

When feeding round bales, you may choose to use a round bale feeder to contain the hay and minimize waste. Make sure you choose one that is designed and marketed specifically for horses. Many are designed for cattle and are not safe for horse use.

Grain and Ration Balancer

"Grain" is the generic term used to describe any type of processed, concentrated feed for horses. It can be in various forms, such as pelleted, extruded, whole (such as whole oats or barley), or a mixture of the above. Grain mixes coated with a layer of molasses are known as sweet feeds.

Not all horses need grain. In fact, the less grain you can feed your horse, the healthier he may be. Large amounts of concentrates can be damaging to the equine digestive tract, leading to such complications as ulcers, colic, and laminitis. However, many horses do benefit from the additional nutrients available in a high-quality grain, fed at a reasonable rate. Such horses include:

- Horses in moderate to hard work.
- Pregnant or lactating mares.

- Young, growing horses.
- Breeding stallions.
- Hard keepers (those with a naturally higher metabolism).
- Senior horses, especially those that have dental problems that make hay difficult to chew.
- Neglected, underweight horses that are being brought back into condition.

If you do choose to feed grain to your horse, I cannot emphasize strongly enough the value of choosing a high-quality product. Cheap grains are often bloated with fillers that are of no nutritional value to the horse. You may end up feeding a much higher quantity of a low-quality grain in order to keep weight on your horse, when a higher quality grain would do the job better at a lower rate of feeding, while providing more appropriate nutrients as well. Think about it—why feed 15 pounds a day of $10-a-bag grain, when you could feed 5 pounds a day of $20-a-bag grain? You will find that you actually end up spending less money, and your horses will be healthier, with a better quality grain.

In any case, be sure never to feed more than 5 pounds of any grain in a single meal. More than 5 pounds can exacerbate or lead to intes-

LEFT: A side benefit of feeding your horses a grain meal is the twice-daily opportunity to look them over for injuries or health problems.

RIGHT: A round-bale feeder appropriate for horses.

tinal distress, as mentioned above. If the horse truly needs more than 10 pounds of grain per day, split the ration into three or more meals, allowing at least four hours between grain meals.

Manufacturers these days are offering a broad range of grain products to meet the needs of a variety of horses. You can find grains formulated for performance horses, seniors, mares and foals, and growing youngsters, as well as specialized products like low-starch (for insulin-resistant horses) and complete feeds (for horses that can't eat hay). Research brands that are available in your area, and choose the best quality product formulated for your specific needs.

High-quality grains are produced such that feeding the recommended minimum amount will provide the correct balance of vitamins, minerals, protein, and micronutrients that horses need. If you are feeding no grain or less than the manufacturer's recommended amount of grain, your horse may not be getting all the nutrients he needs. In that case, you can consider feeding a vitamin/mineral supplement or a ration balancer. Vitamin/mineral supplements are fed as a supplement at a rate of 2 to 3 ounces per day, and can help fill holes in the horse's diet. A ration balancer is a pelleted grainlike product that, in addition to higher levels of nutrients, also provides protein and lysine, a necessary amino acid often deficient in hay-only diets. Ration balancers are usually formulated to balance a specific type of diet—they may be labeled, for example, as "grass balancers" or "alfalfa balancers." Ration balancers—also called diet balancers—are fed at a higher rate than vitamin/mineral supplements, usually 1 to 2 pounds per day.

Pelleted grain product.

What My Horses Eat

I have four horses currently at my farm. Their nutritional needs vary greatly, so each horse's diet is tailored to his or her unique requirements. Robin, our 15.1-hand Appaloosa mare, is a tank and is the very definition of "air fern"—she seems to stay fat on almost no food. She is worked lightly; we trail ride and school low-level dressage three to four times per week. Allegro, our retired boarder and a 16.3 Cleveland Bay/Thoroughbred cross, is also an easy keeper as long as she's getting plenty of forage. She is not in work at all. Beamer, a 16.1-hand Appendix gelding, also does well on good forage, but when he's in regular work, he tends to drop a little weight, so he needs a few extra calories. George is my first horse, a 16.3-hand Thoroughbred with a metabolism supermodels would die for. Although he's retired due to unsoundness, he eats more than all my other horses combined. In addition to plenty of good grass hay or pasture in season, and a daily vitamin E/selenium supplement due to our area's deficiency, here is what I feed them each, twice a day:

Robin 1 cup grass balancer. 1 cup soaked beet pulp.

Allegro 1 cup grass balancer. 1 cup soaked beet pulp.

Beamer 1 cup grass balancer. 1 quart Triple Crown Senior.

George 3 quarts Triple Crown Senior. 3 quarts beet pulp (1 quart pellets measured dry, then soaked). 2 cups rice bran/flax seed high-fat supplement.

Salt and Minerals

All grazing animals need a supplementary source of salt in their diets. To meet this need for your horses, there are several options. The traditional method is to provide them with a salt block, available free-choice at all times. Salt blocks come in several sizes, from 1-pound blocks made for wall-mounted hangers to 5-pound blocks to be placed on the ground in a pan. Be sure to purchase salt blocks that are made for horses and include other essential trace minerals, not just plain white salt.

A newer type of salt that has recently become trendy is Himalayan rock salt. Large chunks of natural salt have been mined from sources in the Himalayas and shipped to the United States for use in cooking as well as feeding to horses. These beautiful pink "rocks" contain natural sources of several trace minerals. They are also quite expensive.

A third option is to offer loose trace minerals to your horses. Loose minerals are easier for the horse to consume than solid blocks of salt that need to be licked—an action that doesn't come naturally to a horse. Loose trace minerals can be offered free-choice, the idea being that the horse will naturally consume the ideal amount for his body's needs.

The bottom line is that no matter which method of salt delivery you choose, it's important to provide free-choice salt to your horses at all times.

BELOW: Himalayan rock salt is often milled into wheel shapes that make the blocks convenient for hanging.

BELOW: The reddish color of this large salt block indicates that it contains trace minerals in addition to salt.

Supplements

Nutritional supplements for equines are a booming business right now. People love to add a little of this and a little of that to their horses' grain bins to feel that they are providing the best possible care. Supplements can be very useful and can help solve many problems that horses have. On the other hand, many horses live long, happy lives without supplements. Consult with your vet when considering adding a new supplement to determine whether it would be beneficial for your horse.

There are hundreds of supplements designed to address a broad range of conditions. A brief list some of the more popular types of supplements is below. For a more in-depth discussion, refer to Eleanor Kellon's *Horse Journal Guide to Equine Supplements and Nutraceuticals*.

Calming. Calming supplements may contain a variety of ingredients designed to support the nervous system and relax the horse. Herbal ingredients often include valerian, raspberry leaf, and chamomile. Spookiness and anxiety in horses have been linked to magnesium deficiency in some cases, so a supplement containing magnesium may be beneficial. Vitamin B1 can also help ease stress. Tryptophan is a naturally occurring calming agent used in many supplements. For mares with hormonal issues, specific calming supplements exist to address those imbalances.

Digestion. Supplements can help address various digestive problems in the horse. Probiotics are live, active cultures that replenish intestinal flora following stress, illness, or antibiotic use. They can also help a horse that is having trouble gaining weight or has diarrhea. Various antacid supplements provide relief to a horse that suffers from ulcers as well.

Hoof. If a horse has hooves that are chronically weak or brittle, it may indicate a nutritional deficiency. Assess the horse's diet to make sure he's getting adequate protein. Supplements containing biotin or the amino acids methionine or lysine help promote healthy hoof growth. Biotin, in particular, has been shown to improve hoof quality even in horses who do not show a clinical deficiency. It takes from nine months to a year for new hoof growth to reach ground level, so you won't see the effects of a supplement instantly.

Joint. Perhaps the most popular type of supplement, especially for performance horses, is joint supplements. Galloping, jumping, sliding, spinning, and turning are all hard on a horse's joints, and over time joint damage can be cumulative and degenerative. Supplements containing such ingredients as glucosamine, chondroitin sulfate, expand MSM (a natural anti-inflammatory), and hyaluronic acid (HA) can help alleviate joint pain and reduce further damage. Many supplements also contain various natural and herbal ingredients to support joint health, such as perna mussel, devil's claw, yucca, and boswellia.

Multivitamin. Most horses don't need a multivitamin supplement, as their dietary needs are being met by grass, hay, grain, or ration balancers. For horses with increased nutritional needs, such as pregnant or lactating mares, elderly horses, or horses being brought back from very poor condition, a multivitamin may be warranted. A multivitamin supplement may be a good choice for a horse that only eats hay or grass, without any ration balancer or grain at all.

Skin and coat. A healthy coat is the result of good management. A coat or fat supplement alone will not do the trick. Feed quality hay, provide fresh water, deworm the horse bimonthly or as recommended by your veterinarian, and groom the horse daily. If a horse's coat has a dull, dry appearance, look first to these basics. But assuming that these conditions have been met, some horses need a little extra nutrition to really bloom.

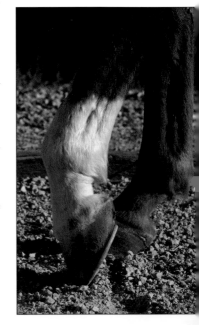

RIGHT: Although hoof health is largely determined by environment and genetics, a hoof supplement can go a long way toward improving horn quality.

Introducing Supplements

Use caution when introducing any new supplement or grain product to your horse's diet. Begin with a small amount, and gradually increase the quantity over a period of several days until you reach the desired amount. (For example, when adding oil, start with two tablespoons, and gradually work up to one cup.) This will allow the horse to become accustomed to the taste, so that he won't reject the new feed entirely, and also allows his digestive system to acclimate to the new nutrients.

Many supplements are served in such small quantities that an acclimation period isn't necessary. However, some, especially joint supplements, have a recommended "loading dose," usually double the amount of the regular dose, to be administered for the first week or two. Follow the instructions on the supplement label, or your veterinarian's advice, regarding loading doses.

Often, simply adding a source of fat to the horse's diet can result in a more pleasing appearance and a shinier coat. Ground flax seed, black oil sunflower seeds, rice bran, or corn or other vegetable oils are all concentrated sources of fat that can help improve coat condition. In other cases, the horse may be lacking in a specific nutrient, such as biotin, selenium, vitamin E, or copper. You can ask your vet to assess the horse's diet and determine whether there may be any specific deficiencies. (Use caution when supplementing with selenium, since too much selenium is toxic.)

Weight Gain. Very hard keepers may require a little something extra to help maintain their weight. See the sidebar above titled "My Horse Is Too Thin" for some ideas to get you started. If you still want to add a supplement, there are a variety of weight gain supplements on the market that offer high amounts of fat and calories in a concentrated package. Rice bran, or rice bran with the addition of ground stabilized flaxseed, is a popular choice.

10. Grooming and Daily Care

The Joy of Grooming

GROOMING IS ONE of the greatest pleasures of horse ownership. Each day offers another opportunity to spend time with your horse, scratching his itches and cleaning his skin and coat while you bond with him. In a herd setting, horses demonstrate their friendship through mutual grooming—nibbling on each other's necks, withers, and backs to clean the coat and scratch itches. When you take the time to groom your horse with care and attention, he will understand that you are showing him affection and friendship. Some horses may even try to reciprocate by nuzzling your hip or shoulder as you brush. (But never allow your horse to contact you with his teeth, even in affection. This type of grooming behavior can quickly escalate to nipping.)

Daily grooming increases circulation to the skin and removes loose hair, dander, and dirt, making the horse gleam with good health. It also offers you an opportunity to assess your horse for any new injuries, scratches, swellings, or skin conditions, and to treat them immediately before they get worse. As you groom, run your hand down each of the horse's legs, feeling for heat or swelling that can indicate an injury.

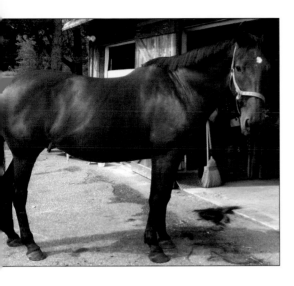

LEFT: The result of a thorough grooming session—a shiny, clean horse.

Pick your horse's hooves daily to make sure they stay clean and free of thrush, as well as to check for foreign objects. Abnormal heat in the hooves can indicate trouble, such as an abscess or the start of laminitis.

Grooming can be a meditative process, allowing you to "get in the zone" and focus fully on what you are doing in the present moment—forget about bills that need paying and chores that need doing; let go of work-related anxiety and family-related stresses. Just groom your horse. Feel his muscles under the curry. Notice when he responds with pleasure as you find those itchy spots, stretching out his neck and curling his lip. Watch with satisfaction as the dust and hair fall away from the coat, leaving it slick and clean. Start with a fuzzy, muddy yak and finish with a gleaming steed.

The Daily Grooming Routine

The daily grooming session is an important ritual. Not only does it keep the horse clean, but it also has many other benefits: Bonding between owner and horse; ground-training and manners refreshers for the horse as needed; an opportunity to check the horse for physical problems such as injuries, swellings, skin problems, weight loss or gain, or behavioral changes; bringing circulation to the skin; lightly massaging the muscles; and distributing the skin's natural oils throughout the coat.

The basic routine is as follows:

LEFT: Horses engage in mutual grooming to express and establish friendship.

1. Using a curry in one hand and a stiff-bristled body brush in the other, knock off any dried clumps of mud. Wet mud is more difficult to remove. It's best to either hose it off or wait for it to dry, and then brush it off. If the horse is shedding heavily in spring, use a shedding blade to remove as much loose hair as possible.

2. Use the curry firmly in small, circular motions over the muscular parts of the horse's body (neck, chest, shoulders, barrel, and haunches). The curry brings to the surface dirt, dry skin, and loose hairs that will later be brushed away.

3. Working from the front of the horse and moving toward the tail, use a medium-bristled body brush in the direction of hair growth to whisk away the debris loosened by the curry. Also use this brush on the legs and belly.

4. Switch to a soft-bristled brush to dust off any remaining debris left by the medium brush. Brush the horse's whole body in the direction of hair growth using short, brisk strokes.

LEFT Picking the front feet.

RIGHT: Picking the hind feet.

BELOW A soft brush provides the finishing touch to the coat.

5. Use a slightly damp washcloth or small towel to rub the horse's face and ears. Then use a small soft brush to set the hair as it dries.

6. Use a different damp cloth or sponge to clean under the horse's tail and between the hind legs as needed.

7. Pick the horse's hooves. Use a pick to remove packed-in dirt, carefully scraping it out from the clefts of the frog and checking for evidence of thrush (black, smelly material). Apply thrush treatment if needed.

8. Finger-comb the tail, removing any bits of hay or bedding. Do not brush or comb the tail unless it has just been washed and conditioned; otherwise you risk breaking the hairs. Comb the mane so that it all hangs on the same side of the neck, and comb the forelock to lie down flat.

9. For special occasions, use a rub rag to finish off the grooming job. Spritz a towel lightly with plain water or water mixed with a grooming product such as Show Sheen or baby oil. Rub the horse's body, removing all specks of dust and loose hair. Finish by using the soft brush to set the hair.

After your ride, brush the horse again with the soft brush to remove any arena dust. If he is just a little sweaty, use a medium-bristled brush on the sweaty areas (usually under the saddle and girth and on the neck) until the horse is dry. If he's very sweaty, hose or sponge off the sweat. After a hard ride on a hot day, a splash of liniment in the bath water is cool and refreshing and helps cut through the sweat. Rinse the neck, chest, saddle and girth area, belly, between the hind legs, and the head. (Be careful not to get any liniment in the horse's eyes.) Use a sweat

scraper to remove as much water as possible, and towel-dry the lower legs to prevent fungus from developing.

The Quick Pre-Ride Grooming Session

You may not always have time for a full grooming session. If you're short on time before a ride, be sure to follow this routine to make sure the horse is comfortable during the ride:

- Brush saddle and girth area with a hard brush.
- Brush mud off legs, being especially careful if you'll be using wraps or boots.
- Pick hooves.
- Check bridle area and brush if needed.

Then just tack up and you're good to go. Be sure to do a thorough grooming the next day.

Hoof Care

Horses' hooves require daily attention. In the case of a shod horse, hoof picking is the one grooming task that should be done *every* day. While cleaning the hoof, check to be sure the shoe is tight and all nails are in place. A loose shoe can twist, causing the horse to step on a nail or clip, or can be ripped off, damaging the hoof wall. Inspect the sole for rocks, bruises, or signs of abscess. Stay alert for evidence of thrush, white line disease, seedy toe, or other problems. Check the outer hoof wall for chips, cracks, and irregularities.

Barefoot horses need slightly less vigilance. There is no risk of a shoe becoming loose or twisted, and the risk of the horse picking up a rock is also reduced. Bare hooves tend to clean themselves out as the horse moves, assuming the environment is relatively dry and clean. Nevertheless, bare hooves should still be checked and picked, if needed, every few days. The barefoot horse may also be at increased risk of sole bruising or hoof wall chipping if he lives or works on rocky terrain.

A variety of products may be used on the horse's hoof, either to increase toughness, moisturize, seal, protect, or disinfect. Keep in mind that the horse's hoof naturally regulates its own moisture level, and adding too much moisture can soften the hoof wall. Hoof ointment should be rubbed into the coronary band because that is where the entire hoof wall grows from, and therefore where the products have some effect.

Thrush is a common condition that affects the clefts of the frog. When hooves are not picked regularly or the horse lives in wet or unsanitary conditions, bacteria can infect the soft tissues of the hoof, causing them to deteriorate. When caught early, thrush is easily treated, but if it becomes too advanced it can become chronic, causing lameness. Thrush produces a soft, black substance and a distinctive foul odor. Prevent or treat it by keeping the horse on dry, clean footing, and picking the hooves daily. Topical application of an anti-thrush product, such as Koppertox or Thrush Buster, can help resolve the problem quickly.

Treating Minor Injuries and Skin Conditions

In your daily grooming sessions, you will encounter the occasional minor laceration or skin irritation. Horses in group turnout situations use their teeth and hooves to communicate and to establish dominance, so it's only natural that a horse will come in with an occasional bite mark. (A horse who regularly gets bitten or kicked, however, should probably be moved to another pasture with more appropriate companions.) A small bite mark or abrasion is nothing to worry about, but treat it immediately to prevent infection or scarring.

Minor Cuts

Horses have quite thick skin, so many wounds simply result in the loss of the hair and top layer of skin. There's no bleeding, and the wound heals very quickly. For these types of injuries, simply clean the area with water and a soft cloth, and apply a thin layer of an ointment like Bag Balm, which moisturizes the tissue to promote healing and creates a barrier against dirt and bacteria.

A deeper wound with bleeding calls for cleaning with an antiseptic scrub such as Betadine. Dry the wound and apply a veterinary antibiotic ointment. Repeat this treatment daily until the wound heals. Wounds on the lower legs require extra attention, since they are closer to the ground and are exposed to bacteria in the soil and manure. A minor skin injury on a lower leg can easily become a serious infection. The fungal disease known as scratches can quickly take hold. Consider wrapping the injury with cotton batting and a standing wrap if the injury is large or actively bleeding. Call the vet if you aren't sure what to do or if the injury starts to look infected (inflamed, hot, and possibly oozing pus).

Note: A puncture wound involving a joint is a very serious injury. Call your vet immediately. If the puncture penetrates the joint capsule, severe infection can set in very quickly and can be life-threatening. Any injury to the eye or a puncture wound in the sole of the hoof (as from stepping on a nail) is also cause for an immediate call to the vet due to the severe risks associated with infection.

That's a Wrap

Knowing how to wrap horses' legs properly is an important skill. Wrapping is useful in a variety of situations, but it must be done correctly or it can cause injury due to uneven pressure on the delicate tendons of the lower leg. This is something that you should learn from your instructor, trainer, or even your vet, as it is a hands-on skill that really can't be learned from a book. Practice often! The basic steps are as follows:

1. Assemble your materials: Rolled padding material (roll cotton or thick pillow wraps) and rolled standing wraps or VetWrap.

2. Align the pillow wrap along the horse's leg such that it will unroll across the front of the cannon bone. Begin to unroll it, keeping a firm and consistent pressure with both hands.

3. Once you have wrapped all of the padding material evenly around the leg, insert the end of the rolled standing wrap approximately in the middle of the pillow wrap such that the standing wrap will unroll in the same direction as the pillow wrap.

4. Make one turn of the standing wrap around the leg, not too tight, overlapping the beginning of your standing wrap to hold it in place.

5. Begin to work your way up the leg as you unroll the standing wrap, being careful to maintain an even tension and avoid any wrinkles in the fabric.

6. When there's about an inch of pillow wrap left showing at the top of the wrap, work your way back down to the bottom of the wrap, leaving an inch or so of pillow wrap revealed at the bottom as well.

7. Proceed back up to the middle of the wrap where you started. At this point you should reach the end of the standing wrap. Use the Velcro at the end of the wrap to secure it in place.

The key is to maintain a constant, even, firm (but not too tight) pressure as you wrap. Always remove and rewrap daily to check the status of the underlying condition and to refresh the soiled wraps.

When to use standing wraps:

- To cover, protect, and hold medication in place over a laceration on the lower leg.
- To prevent stocking up or swelling of the lower legs.
- Over a poultice.
- When one leg is injured, wrap both legs to provide support to the uninjured leg, which will be bearing more weight.
- To provide protection when trailering.

Skin Conditions

Horses are prone to a number of skin conditions, from allergic reactions to fungal infections. Some of the most common are hives, rain rot, and scratches (pastern dermatitis).

Hives are raised welts on the horse's skin, and are caused by an allergic reaction. They may be caused by a new type of feed, an insect, or something in the horse's environment. They may be itchy or not. For first aid, witch hazel or calamine lotion applied topically can help soothe the itch. In the long term, you'll need to identify the source of the allergy and remove it. For example, if it is insects, try using a different type of fly spray or a fly sheet, or perhaps even bring the horse into his stall at the time of day when the offending insects are feeding.

Rain rot is a fungal infection that typically affects the skin of the back, hindquarters, and neck and is commonly seen in neglected or malnourished horses. It presents as black or gray, scaly patches and hair loss on the affected areas. The direct cause is exposure to too much moisture (as from being left out in the rain) combined with too little grooming and inadequate nutrition to allow the body's immune system to function well. Clean thoroughly, treat with topical antifungal ointments, groom regularly, and protect the horse from rain while he heals. Review his diet and consider changing it, increasing it, or adding a vitamin/mineral supplement to make sure he is getting everything he needs.

Scratches is the common name of a fungal infection of the pasterns and fetlocks. You will notice raised bumps on the skin, developing into crusty scabs that are painful when picked at. Scratches can spread quickly, and left untreated can become quite severe, causing generalized inflammation of the lower limbs. It is caused by wet, unsanitary conditions, usually with horses standing in muddy, manure-filled paddocks, although even horses in drier conditions can get it. Some horses seem to be naturally more susceptible, and have to be treated preventatively to make sure they don't develop scratches each spring. For such a horse, keep the fetlock hair clipped short, make sure his living environment is dry and clean, and be sure to dry the lower legs any time they become wet.

To treat an existing case of scratches, bathe the affected area with an antiseptic scrub, dry thoroughly, and coat the scabby area in an ointment such as ichthammol, and leave it on overnight. This will penetrate and moisturize the scabs, allowing them to be picked off more easily. The next day, repeat the scrubbing, attempting to remove any scabs that will come off. Be careful, and be aware that the process may be painful for the horse. If some scabs are too painful to remove, leave them alone and repeat the ichthammol dressing and scrubbing cycle. Another option is to create a homemade remedy made from equal parts triple antibiotic ointment, zinc oxide diaper rash cream,

LEFT: The first step in treating any skin condition is usually to wash the area with an antibiotic or antifungal shampoo.

and Monistat yeast infection treatment. Smear this paste onto the affected area twice daily. Before each application, gently wipe off any accumulated residue, but do not wash or scrub. Keep applying this treatment until all sign of infection is gone and new hair is growing back normally. It may take several days to clear up the infection. Be vigilant, and keep the horse in a dry area in between treatments. If scratches, or any other skin condition, does not begin to clear up after several days of treatment, call your vet for further advice.

Rain rot, scratches, and other fungal infections like thrush are signs that you may need to review your horsekeeping practices. Is your paddock too muddy? Do you pick out your run-in shed daily, or is it full of manure? Is there enough clean, dry bedding in your stalls? Do you groom your horses and pick their feet often enough? Perhaps most fundamentally, is your nutrition program up to par? If a horse is not getting enough to eat, or if his diet is lacking in the necessary vitamins and minerals, his immune system can suffer, allowing fungal infections to take hold. These types of infections can serve as the canary in the coal mine—letting you know that something is amiss before the problem becomes even more severe.

BELOW: An especially nasty case of scratches.

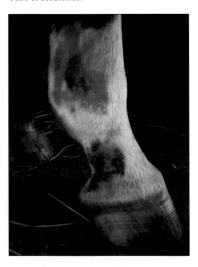

ABOVE: To help prevent scratches from developing on a horse that is prone to the infection, towel-dry the legs thoroughly anytime they become wet.

Bathing

You will not need to bathe your horse daily, or even weekly. In fact, it is best not to bathe too often, since shampoos can remove beneficial oils from the horse's coat and dry the skin. Nevertheless, it is an important grooming skill. Horses that do not show should be bathed at least a few times a year. Show horses may be bathed before every show.

It is best not to bathe the horse if the ambient temperature is below 60 degrees, as the wet horse can catch a chill. The best day for a bath is a dry, sunny day in the 70s or 80s. In chilly weather, be sure to cover the horse with a cooler after his bath until he is dry.

Any time the horse's legs become wet, whether it is due to a bath, a cold-hosing session, or a swim in a pond, it is important to dry them as thoroughly as possible. First use your hands to scrape the water off, and then use a clean, dry towel to rub the lower legs. If the legs remain wet, they are susceptible to a variety of fungal infections. In addition, the skin around the pasterns may crack, leading to infection.

Bath time!

What You'll Need

- Bucket
- Water source (such as a hose)
- Shampoo and conditioner
- Sponge
- Curry or stiff brush with nylon bristles
- Sweat scraper
- Towels
- Tail detangler
- Cooler

  For a full bath, the procedure is as follows:

1. Squirt some horse shampoo into a 5-gallon bucket and fill with warm water.
2. Soak the horse with a hose.
3. Scrub a quarter of the horse (say, the neck, shoulder, front leg, and barrel on the left side) with the warm, soapy water using a sponge, nylon-bristled brush, or curry.
4. Rinse thoroughly with the hose, and scrape with a sweat scraper. If any soap bubbles appear, rinse again.
5. Move to the hindquarters and back leg on the same side and repeat steps 3 and 4.
6. Repeat steps 3 and 4 on the right front and then right hind. (Change the bath water at some point if the horse is quite dirty.)
7. Use a smaller sponge or washcloth to gently bathe the face. Rinse the washcloth in clean water and use it to remove the suds. (Do not spray the horse's face with the hose.) If the horse will tolerate it, you can let the hose water run gently from the top of the head so the water trickles down the face to rinse it.
8. Lather and rinse the tail, being careful to remove all traces of soap residue to avoid itching.
9. Apply a conditioner to the horse's coat and tail. Some conditioners are meant to be rinsed off, while others are leave-in products. Follow the directions on the bottle.

10. Towel dry the legs, and in chilly weather cover the horse with a fleece or wool cooler. When the horse is dry, brush him with a clean, soft brush to set the hair.

Sheets and Blankets

Not every horse needs a blanket in the winter. Several factors influence the choice of whether or not to blanket: climate, available shelter, breed, age, body condition, the thickness of the natural coat, and whether or not the horse is clipped. An elderly Thoroughbred in poor weight who lives outdoors in Vermont definitely needs a blanket in the winter. A fat, furry Shetland living in a stable in Virginia probably does not. Any horse that is clipped needs additional protection from the elements, since you've taken away his natural insulation.

There are a variety of different types and weights of blanket. "Denier" refers to the thread count of the outer shell of the blanket. A higher denier generally means a more durable blanket. For turnout blankets, look for a denier of at least 1200. A stable blanket will have a much lower denier, since it will only be used in the stall and won't be subjected to weather and horseplay. Insulation is measured in grams. A blanket with 100 to 200 grams of fill is a light- or medium-weight blanket adequate for most needs. A heavyweight blanket with more than 300 grams of fill is best for clipped horses or very cold weather.

Turnout blankets should be waterproof and breathable. This means that they will keep rain out, but will allow moisture from the horse's body to evaporate through the blanket, keeping the horse dry underneath.

When to Blanket

Living in Maine, with our frigid winters, I like to keep three blanket choices for each horse—a waterproof turnout sheet, a light- or medium-weight turnout blanket, and a heavyweight turnout blanket. I don't bother with stable blankets, since my horses live outside. (Stable blankets should never be used outdoors, since they're not waterproof. If it rains or snows, the blanket will become soaked, and the horse can get very cold. It's better for a horse to have no blanket at all than to wear one that's soaked through.)

Turnout sheets are unlined, so they don't offer any extra insulation, but they serve as effective windbreakers and raincoats. I use turnout sheets for rainy or snowy weather when it's colder than about 50 degrees Fahrenheit. (If it's not precipitating or windy, I don't use a sheet in these temperatures. A sheet can flatten down the hair and actually make the horse colder.) When the temperature drops below 25, I change to medium-weight blankets to add a little extra warmth. Below zero, I use heavyweight blankets. On those bitterly cold January nights when it's 15 below zero, I layer a medium and heavyweight blanket together.

Blanketing is a very personal decision, and your choices will depend heavily on your local environment and what your own horses prefer. Keep an eye on your herd as the temperature drops, and add blankets if they look cold. A cold horse will be standing stiffly, with his back hunched and rump turned toward the wind, with tail tucked and ears back. He may even shiver. Horsekeepers' wisdom tell us to feel the horse's ears—if the ears feel cold, the horse is cold.

On warm days, remove the blankets to let the horses have a roll in the snow. I pull blankets on any sunny winter day above 20 degrees or so. If it gets warm enough that they may sweat under the blankets, they should definitely be removed. A sweaty, blanketed horse is itchy and uncomfortable, and when the sun goes down in the evening he'll be wet and cold. Generally speaking, they're better off a little too cold than too warm, so if there's any doubt, always err on the side of fewer blankets rather than more.

Blanket Selection and Care

Blankets are another item where buying cheap is definitely a false economy. It's worthwhile to do some research and read reviews online before deciding on a brand. Don't just buy the least expensive blankets in the tack catalog. You'll regret it, as they'll tear more easily, the insulation will flatten out, and they'll lose their waterproofing. You'll have to buy a new blanket in just a year or two. Top quality blankets can last a decade or more with good care. Some of the brands with which I've had the best luck are Rambo and Weatherbeeta. Rambos are quite pricy, but the quality is truly unsurpassed. Weatherbeetas are a more affordable, yet still durable, option.

Any blanket you choose will need care. Daily care is minimal—just check for tears so you can repair them before they get worse, and knock off any encrusted mud with a hard brush if you like. If weather allows, you can hang a dirty blanket over a fence and hose it off. If a blanket gets wet on the outside, as long as the waterproofing is intact and the lining doesn't get wet all the way through, it will dry most quickly if you just leave it on the horse. A truly soaked blanket needs to be removed and hung to dry in a warm place. Never leave a blanket that is wet underneath on a horse. In wet weather, I run my hand under each blanket daily to make sure they are keeping the horses dry.

At the end of the season, all blankets should be cleaned, dried, repaired if necessary, and stored in a secure location, protected from insects, rodents, and moisture. Many home washing machines are not large enough or heavy-duty enough to handle horse blankets. If yours is, be sure you wash your blankets in cold water with a detergent specially made for horse blankets. Don't use regular laundry detergent, as it can damage the waterproofing. Do up all the buckles and Velcro before washing. Hang the blankets to dry after washing, and then fold and store them in plastic bags or storage bins.

Personally, I prefer to bring my blankets to a professional for washing and repair. It's more expensive than doing it myself, but it's so much easier, and I don't have to worry about damage to my washing machine. My blankets come back spotlessly clean, carefully folded, and professionally repaired, and I feel good knowing I'm supporting an equine professional in my community.

Day Branch Farm

Emma Day Branch is a recent high school graduate who, along with her mother Katey Branch, keeps two Arabian mares at her home. Although the mares, Kia and Star, are not related, they look exactly alike. Emma grew up riding her mother's horse, Colonel. After Colonel died when Emma was seven, she wanted a horse of her own. But Katey wisely insisted that Emma learn how to do all of the work that goes along with having a horse. When Emma was ten, Katey arranged for her to start taking lessons and working at a local boarding stable. She worked there for two years before Katey agreed that she was ready to take on the responsibilities of having her own horse. "I think it's really important that she had me do that, because there's really been a love that has grown from that, a connection with horses beyond riding," Emma notes. "Kia has been lame off and on, and it's fine because I just enjoy being around the horses, I don't necessarily need to ride them."

At first, the family kept Kia at home in their large pasture, with a stall in the barn to which she had free access. But Kia wasn't happy alone, and made it clear that she needed to be around other horses in order to thrive. So Emma moved her to the local boarding stable. Emma recalls that there were pros and cons to boarding Kia. "There's a lot less responsibility, and in the winter I could ride because of the indoor, so that's a really big plus. On the downside, there's a bit of a disconnect because you don't see them every day." As a high school student, it was convenient for her to have someone else caring for Kia's daily needs, but the distance kept her away from her beloved mare. "The barn was half an hour away, so it was hard to get out there as much as I wanted to. Plus, my mom and I wanted to ride together, and scheduling time for us both to go out there together was impossible in our lives." When another boarder at the stable left for college, she offered Star to the family as a companion for Kia and riding horse for Katey.

All the responsibilities for daily care of the two horses now fell to Emma, but she relished the work. "I think all that responsibility is good because it strengthens the connection and it's part of what having a horse is all about—being there every day and seeing them every morning and evening and sometimes all afternoon." The mark of any true horse lover, Emma honestly enjoys the work of caring for her animals. "I love, *love* cleaning out stalls," she says with a giggle. "There's something about having Kia just standing there staring at me and I have to keep her out. You can have a conversation with her while you're doing it."

In addition, having her horses at home allowed Emma to experience her own surroundings in a way she would not otherwise have done. "Being able to explore the trail system around here has been really cool," she says. "I've been learning a lot about this area via horseback. I love riding bareback. There's just something really special about it."

I asked Emma what it was like to be a busy high school student and also have a horse. When Kia was boarded at the stable, she recalls, "it was definitely hard. I'd go through phases. It's a habit. Sometimes I'd get into a phase of going out [to the barn] more often. Without her being at home, there's not this constant reminder of a horse that you need to brush and ride and pay attention to. She was off in this detached world. If I could have done it, I would have kept her at home the whole time. Even if I don't have time to ride, I at least feed her and brush her and spend time with her."

Horses have given Emma a unique kind of solace and comfort during her adolescence, which is a difficult time for any young person, and has had its own set of challenges for Emma. During our conversation she recalled a particularly poignant moment with her two mares: "If I'm upset about something, I can go out to the barn and have all the dogs with me, so I have all my animals around me. The horses stick their little heads in for treats. It's just really comforting. One time not that long ago, it was a full moon, and I wanted to go visit my Dad at his grave in the far pasture. Both of the horses stuck right with me, one at each shoulder, and walked out with me and stayed with me the whole time. I think horses are very empathetic."

Winter Grooming

Winter is a season with its own unique set of horsekeeping challenges, and grooming is no exception. During the winter, horses grow a thick, long coat to protect themselves from cold and precipitation. If they are not being worked, it's best to leave that coat alone as much as possible. It should not be clipped or brushed too much. A thick-coated horse may not even need a blanket except in extreme weather.

On the other hand, if the horse remains in work through the cold season, it is best to clip part or all of the coat and blanket the horse. When the horse is ridden, he works up a sweat and a long coat can make him overheat. After the ride, a full winter coat can take hours to dry fully, leaving the horse susceptible to chills. It is healthier for the horse, as well as easier for the groom, to clip. The most common type of clip is a trace clip, in which the long hair is removed only from the sweatiest parts of the horse—the underside of his neck, chest, and belly—leaving the thick coat for warmth over the rest of the horse's body.

Hooves also require special attention in winter. Again, if the horse has the winter off, the natural approach may be best—bare

hooves have better traction and resist ice buildup compared to shod hooves. If the horse remains in work and keeps his shoes on, care must be taken to prevent slipping and "snowballing." Your farrier can add small droplets of metal—called borium—to the bottom of the horse's shoes for added traction if needed.

Feed horses extra hay during cold or wet weather. Digesting the hay produces heat energy that helps keep the horse warm.

LEFT: This pony has been trace-clipped to prevent overheating when he works, as well as to allow sweat to evaporate more quickly when he's done.

Cleaning Sheaths and Udders

Sheath cleaning: The dirty underbelly of the horsekeeping world—literally. Most of us don't relish the task of cleaning a sheath, but it must be done. Frequency depends on the horse. Some geldings seem to stay fairly clean without much cleaning at all, while others need to be cleaned monthly. Signs that a gelding may need his sheath cleaned include tail rubbing, difficulty urinating, and visible smegma. Even if the penis and sheath look pretty clean, the horse should be checked periodically for the presence of a bean—a ball of hard, waxy gray material that develops in the tip of the penis, and can block the urethra and interfere with urination if it becomes too large.

Start with a bucket of lukewarm, clean water and a small clean sponge. A cleaning product, such as Excalibur sheath cleaner, baby oil, or a gentle liquid hand soap, will make the job easier. Wear latex medical gloves for sanitary and aesthetic purposes. Using a wet sponge with a dollop of cleanser, reach into the sheath and gently scrub off any smegma that you find.

If the horse will tolerate it, a low-pressure hose can be used to rinse the sheath after cleaning it.

Mares are much easier, but they too can develop smegma around their udders. A buildup of smegma around or between the udders can be itchy and irritating and can even lead to infection. Like geldings, some mares need to be cleaned often, while others rarely if ever need attention in that area. Do a full scrub-and-clean, as with a gelding, once or twice a year, or as needed. Cleaning udders is a simpler and less invasive task than cleaning a sheath. Use caution, since many mares are very sensitive in this area. Stand well clear of the hind legs, and stay alert for kick warnings from the horse. Gently lather the udders with your cleaning product (use the same product as you'd use for a sheath), using your sponge to carefully scrub all crevices and hidden areas. Rinse the sponge in clean, lukewarm water and wash away all soapy residue. Keep a box of baby wipes in your grooming kit to touch things up between cleanings.

Many horse owners choose not to clean their geldings' sheaths, opting instead to have the vet perform the task. In some cases this is simply a personal choice for owners who find the process distasteful. Some geldings object strenuously to the process, so trying to clean the sheath is unsafe for the owner. Another benefit to having the vet do it is that the vet will most likely administer a sedative that will both calm the horse and cause the muscles around the sheath to relax, allowing the penis to drop down. This way, the vet can do a more thorough cleaning without the risk of being kicked.

Fly Protection

During the warmer months, flies and other biting insects can be a major irritation. Stock up on a good fly spray, and use it daily. Try a variety of brands to find out which works best against the flies in your area. Fly masks with ears are very useful in protecting the horse's head and face. They also ward against eye infections that can be transmitted by flies that feed on the eye's discharge. For a very sensitive horse, use a good-quality fly sheet. (A cheap one will be torn to shreds in no time. Ask me how I know.) A final line of defense is to use a feed-through fly control product containing garlic, which makes the horse's scent unpalatable to flies. I use this type of supplement on a horse that is very sensitive to fly bites and develops hives easily.

Fly predators are a relatively recent innovation in the war against flies. Order them through the mail, and they arrive in paper bags to be distributed at fly breeding sites, such as the manure pile, around your property. They are tiny, stingless wasps that feed on the pupae of flies, preventing them from hatching into adults.

RIGHT: Fly masks protect horses' eyes from irritation.

11. Veterinary Care and Hoof Maintenance

Routine Care

THE HORSE'S PRIMARY caregiver for medical needs is his owner. You are responsible for the routine activities that keep your horse safe and healthy, and you are responsible for recognizing the signs of illness or injury that require a professional's assistance. The most important factors for keeping a horse injury- and illness-free are a safe, clean environment and good nutrition. Horses exemplify a type of Murphy's law—if there is a way to hurt themselves, they will do so. Ensure that their stalls, barn, paddock, and pasture are free of sharp, protruding surfaces. Common culprits are loose nails or screws, loose fence boards, uncapped steel T-posts, and barbed wire or high-tensile wire fence. Check fences and stalls regularly for any signs of disrepair, and fix them immediately. Obviously, all turnout areas should be free of "junk" such as old farm equipment or garbage of any kind.

The horse's diet and lifestyle should combine to keep him as healthy and stress-free as possible. A nutritious, high-quality diet combined with plenty of turnout for exercise and companionship serves most horses well.

Nevertheless, even under the most idyllic of conditions, horses will inevitably require medical attention. Know the signs of illness, such as colic, ulcers, laminitis, influenza, strangles, and other disorders, and know when it is time to call the vet. Learn to take your horse's vital signs so you can quickly provide the vet with this perti-nent information when you call. Many minor injuries can be treated in the barn, without calling in a veterinarian, but there are specific cases in which you must call a vet for assistance, including severe colic, laminitis, choke, lameness with an unknown cause, neurologi-cal symptoms, fever, dehydration, infected wounds or eyes, or severe wounds. When in doubt, call the vet. He or she should be able to assess the situation over the phone and advise you on the best course of action—whether to instruct you on how to treat the problem on your own, to schedule a visit in the near future, to make an emergency farm call, or to trailer the horse to the nearest equine hospital.

Top Ten Equine Veterinary Emergencies

If your horse has any of these conditions, call your vet imme-diately. This is not an exhaustive list of emergencies. If you're unsure how to handle a medical situation or feel you're in over your head, call your vet. When in doubt, call your vet.

1. Colic. This is the leading cause of death in horses, and can progress quickly from a mild to life-threatening condition.
2. Acute lameness. If your horse is very lame and you don't know why, call your vet. Lameness can signify a number of serious conditions requiring veterinary intervention, including frac-tures, punctures in the hoof, laminitis, or soft tissue injury.
3. Choke. In this condition, the horse's esophagus has become blocked with food. Thanks to the design of the horse's esopha-gus, unlike humans, the horse can still breathe, but cannot swallow. He may appear to be in great distress, with green froth coming from his mouth or nose.

4. Lacerations and punctures. Deep lacerations and punctures may require veterinary attention in the form of cleaning, suturing, and administering antibiotics.

5. Joint and tendon injuries. If a laceration or puncture involves a joint or tendon, it is even more important to get prompt medical attention, since infections in these areas can be devastating.

6. Eye trauma or infection. Without immediate treatment, it is possible for injury or infection to lead to vision loss, or even loss of the entire eye itself. If you observe that an eye is swollen, closed, or is emitting discharge, consider it an emergency.

7. Exertional myopathy (tying up). When a horse is pushed beyond its physical limits, its back and hindquarter muscles may "tie up," or become extremely tight and hard. The horse will appear to be in great discomfort and may be unwilling or unable to move. Veterinary treatment is required to prevent renal problems.

8. Reproductive emergencies. Although most broodmares deliver their foals without complications, in cases when problems do occur things can get very bad very quickly, potentially leading to the loss of the foal, the dam, or both. Call your vet immediately.

9. Foal emergencies. As newborns, foals are more susceptible to a variety of diseases and illnesses. Call your vet right away if your foal seems sick.

10. ADRs. This is vet-speak for "ain't doin' right," also known as NQR, or "not quite right." There is no shame in calling the vet because you just sense that there is something wrong with your horse, even though you can't place your finger on just what it is. You know your horse better than anyone, and if you suspect there's something amiss, you're probably right.

Source: Adapted from www.bendequine.com/documents/TopTen EquineEmergencies.pdf.

Equine Vital Signs

Sign	Normal Range	How to check
Temperature	99–100.5°F	Rectal thermometer
Heart Rate	24–44	Find the pulse under the jaw, or use a stethoscope at the girth
Respiratory Rate	8–20	Count the number of breaths per minute
Mucous Membrane	Moist and pink	Visually inspect the gums
Capillary Refill Time	Under 2 seconds	Press the gums with a thumb until the spot turns white; count the number of seconds for pink color to return

Common veterinary conditions you may be able to handle yourself

Hoof abscess. Many instances of acute lameness are caused by hoof abscesses. The horse may suddenly appear to be severely lame, even unable to bear weight on the affected hoof, as abscesses can be extremely painful. The hoof wall or sole may feel hot or warm to the touch, especially near the precise location of the abscess. Slight puffiness of the pastern and fetlock may accompany the heat and pain. If you are sure you're dealing with an abscess and not a more serious injury, you can treat it yourself by soaking the hoof in hot water and Epsom salts, and wrapping the hoof with a poultice of ichthammol or Epsom salts packed into the sole. This will soften the sole and encourage the infection to drain downward. Avoid using bute unless the horse is in so much pain he can't walk to water and food; its anti-inflammatory action can actually prevent the abscess from bursting and hence resolving. Keep him turned out in a safe paddock with friendly companions so he can move around, which helps the abscess to progress. If the horse is extremely uncomfortable or the abscess does not seem to improve rapidly, call your vet or farrier. They will be able to identify the exact location of the abscess, and use a sharp tool to open a tract in the sole to drain the infection and relieve the pressure inside the hoof. This will result in immediate pain relief for the horse, although you will need to continue soaking and wrapping the hoof until the infection is gone. If an apparent abscess takes a very long time to resolve and the vet can't locate the exact source of the pain, consider additional diagnostics such as X-rays or ultrasound. Occasionally a more serious injury, such as a suspensory tear or a fracture within the hoof, can masquerade as an abscess, or the abscess itself can progress to infection of the bones in the hoof, which is a very serious condition.

Mild colic. Colic is a difficult condition to deal with emotionally, as it can be extremely mild and resolve on its own in a short period of time, or it can rapidly escalate into a life-threatening condition. One just never knows which way things will go. The signs of colic include the horse acting restless, kicking or biting at his abdomen, sweating, lying down and getting up repeatedly, rolling, thrashing, and refusing food. Treat any colic as a potential medical emergency. Even if the horse is only showing mild signs of discomfort, call your vet right away to put him "on alert" that you have a developing situation and may be needing help, depending on how things go. He will advise you as to the best course of action. (If the horse seems to be in severe pain, call your vet to come to the farm *immediately*. There is no time to waste.) For a mild colic, keep the horse on his feet to prevent him from rolling. Listen to his abdomen on both sides to see if you can hear sounds indicating gut motility, and try to assess whether the horse has been passing manure. Gut sounds and fresh, moist manure are good signs. Intestinal silence and absence of manure indicate that you may be dealing with an impaction or twist, which can be fatal. If the horse will walk quietly with you and you hear gut sounds, a dose of Banamine and hand-walking can help resolve the situation without a vet's assistance. Call your vet immediately if the horse's condition starts to worsen.

Skin conditions. Most skin conditions, such as rain rot and scratches (a fungal infection of the pastern and fetlock area characterized by black scabs, hair loss, and cracking of the skin), can be treated by using medicated shampoos and ointments. If the condition worsens or does not improve within a few days, call your vet for advice. Skin infections can be a sign of reduced immune response due to a nutritional imbalance or deficiency, so assess your horse's diet and make sure he's getting what he needs.

Home Remedy for Scratches

1 tube Desitin diaper rash cream—40 percent zinc

1 tube Monistat 7

1 tube triple antibiotic ointment

You can purchase all of these ingredients at your local pharmacy. The Monistat 7 addresses the primary fungal infection, while the triple antibiotic treats any secondary bacterial infection and the Desitin holds everything together, makes it stick to the leg, and keeps out environmental moisture. Mix them together into a thick paste and apply it to the affected area twice daily. Do not wash or scrub. Gently wipe off the accumulated ointment with a soft, dry towel before each new application; soon the scratches scabs will start to come off as well. Do not pick or scrub them off—they will come off easily when they're ready. Continue treatment until all the skin looks healthy and new hair has started to regrow. If the condition does not improve or worsens, call your vet.

Thrush. Thrush is a fungal hoof infection of the tissues of the sole and frog, evidenced by thick, black material and a distinctive foul odor. Treat it by picking the hoof daily and applying a topical thrush treatment. Treat thrush promptly, as it can develop into a painful and persistent condition. Be sure the horse is living in clean, dry conditions. Mud, manure buildup, and dirty stalls or pens quickly lead to thrush, so take a case of thrush as a sign to review your horse management practices.

Minor wounds. Horses often come in from the pasture with minor skin wounds. These may be caused by bites or kicks from a pasture-mate, from scratching against or rolling on a sharp object such as a fencepost or rock, or from any number of unknown sources. The good news is, the majority of these wounds are easy to treat on your own. For a very shallow wound that is not bleeding, simply apply a smear of mild ointment such as Bag Balm and send the horse on his merry way. A slightly deeper wound that involves blood should be scrubbed gently with an antibacterial cleanser, such as Betadine or Nolvasan, and coated with antibacterial ointment. Treat wounds on the lower legs with extra caution. Since they are so close to the ground, they are exposed to all sorts of bacteria and fungi and can easily become infected. Scrub, treat, and wrap them daily until they've healed.

If a wound is actively bleeding and won't stop, seems very deep, is a puncture-type wound, or involves a joint, the sole of the hoof, or an eye, call your vet immediately. These types of injuries can be more serious than they appear, and the consequences of severe infection are dire.

Minor swelling of the legs. A slight inflammation or "filling" of the lower legs, unaccompanied by heat or lameness, is known as "stocking up." Often caused by immobility, such as when a horse is stalled for several hours, it is generally harmless and can usually be resolved by a combination of cold-hosing, exercise (such as turnout, hand-walking the horse, or riding), and, if necessary, wrapping the horse's legs if he must be stalled for a period of time. The best remedy for stocking up is simply to let the horse stay outside, where he can move freely and keep the lymphatic fluids moving through his tissues.

Swelling in one leg accompanied by heat and/or lameness usually has a more serious cause, such as a soft tissue injury. Call your vet for an assessment to determine the injury that is causing the inflammation.

Deworming

There are a wide variety of internal parasites that can afflict horses, including roundworms, pinworms, large and small strongyles, bot fly larvae, and tapeworms. They are in the soil, grass, and manure that surround horses, and horses accidentally ingest their eggs or larvae while eating from the ground. The worms then complete their life cycle by hatching inside the host's intestinal system, breeding, and laying more eggs, which the horse then excretes in his manure to start the cycle over again. All horses carry some intestinal parasites, and for the most part they are not harmful. If left unattended, however, a horse's worm burden can grow to the point that it starts affecting the horse's ability to maintain weight and condition. Elderly, underfed, or very young horses are at highest risk. A "wormy" horse appears gaunt and rough-coated with a distinctive enlarged abdomen.

For decades, the conventional horse wisdom has been to deworm all horses every other month, and to rotate dewormers to kill all the different types of parasites. Many horse owners still deworm this way, and it is effective. Recent research, however, has suggested that routine deworming may be leading to dewormer-resistant parasites. A new method called targeted deworming is now being recommended by many vets. In this system, a vet performs annual fecal egg counts on all horses in the herd, and recommends specific dewormers based on which types of parasites are found, in what quantities, and in which

ROTATION DEWORMING SCHEDULE

Month	Active Ingredient
January/February	Pyrantel
March/April	Benzimidazole
May/June	Ivermectin
July/August	Pyrantel
September/October	Benzimidazole
November/December	Ivermectin

horses. Some horses may be found to be "heavy shedders," with lots of worm eggs in their manure, while others in the same herd have almost none. For more information on targeted deworming, see page 164.

If you decide to go with traditional rotation deworming, follow a schedule similar to the one above. A variety of dewormer brands are available on the market for each type of active ingredient.

Vaccinations and Coggins Testing

Like people and house pets, horses need to be vaccinated against several diseases. Discuss with your vet which vaccinations are recommended for your geographic region. Some vaccinations, such as rabies, may be required by law, while others are optional and may depend on the horse's lifestyle. For example, in a stable herd in which the horses never leave the farm and no new horses are expected to come in, an owner may choose not to administer a strangles vaccine, since the chances of the horses contracting strangles is so low.

Although your specific choices may vary based on region and lifestyle, the American Association of Equine Practitioners recommends the following vaccinations for adult horses (over one year old). (Recommendations differ for broodmares and foals.) Core vaccines are recommended for all equines, while risk-based vaccines are optional, based on risk of exposure.

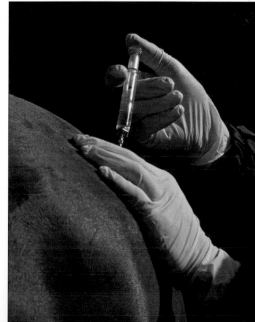

RIGHT: A vet administers annual vaccinations.

CORE VACCINES

Disease	Frequency	Notes
Tetanus	Annual	Booster at time of penetrating injury
Eastern/Western Equine Encephalomyelitis (EEE/WEE)	Annual	Spring
West Nile Virus (WNV)	Annual	Spring
Rabies	Annual	

RISK-BASED VACCINES

Disease	Frequency	Notes
Anthrax	Annual	Booster at time of penetrating injury
Botulism	Annual	Consider vaccinating if you feed round bales
Equine Herpesvirus (EHV)	Annual	Semi-annual for show or breeding horses at high risk
Equine Viral Arteresis (EVA)	Annual	For breeding stallions and mares
Influenza	Annual	Semi-annual for show horses at high risk
Potomac Horse Fever (PHF)	Semi-annual to annual	3- or 4-month interval in endemic areas
Strangles	Semi-annual to annual	
Source: www.aaep.org/images/files/Adultvaccinationtablerevised 108.pdf		

While your veterinarian is administering spring shots, it's also a good time to have him pull a blood sample for a Coggins test. This is a test for equine infectious anemia, a deadly rotavirus that infects horses in the United States. Proof of a negative Coggins test is generally required at all horse shows and for any horse being transported across interstate boundaries. At this point, the disease has nearly been eradicated, and a positive Coggins test is extremely rare. Nonetheless, if you plan to show, board, or move your horse, you will need to have this test performed.

Hoof Care

In addition to checking and picking hooves out several times a week or each time you ride, you'll need to schedule regular visits with a farrier or barefoot trimmer. Depending on the horse's conformation and rate of hoof growth, his hooves need to be trimmed and re-shod every five to eight weeks.

There is much controversy in the horse world over which is better: barefoot or shod. What it comes down to, as for most other horse-keeping decisions, is what is best for the individual horse. Many horses do extremely well barefoot, and in general barefoot hooves tend to be somewhat healthier, since they are self-cleaning and can expand and contract naturally each time the horse takes a step, increasing circulation to the lower legs and hooves as well as acting as a shock absorber for the horse's entire body.

On the other hand, some horses are simply not comfortable bare-foot. They may have conformational problems such as thin soles, flat soles, or thin hoof walls that make their feet more sensitive or delicate. The shoeing decision may also be based on the horse's job. Eventers, fox hunters, and jumpers often need to wear studs in their shoes for traction when jumping on grassy surfaces, and for this they need shoes. Horses that jump or perform reining movements such as sliding stops and spins may benefit from specialized shoeing that helps support them in their work. Many dressage riders feel that shoes help their horses have the best gaits possible.

So, there are pros and cons to either choice. If you are considering adding or removing your horse's shoes, discuss the options with your vet and farrier or trimmer. Don't commit yourself philosophically to one way or the other. Try both, and see which helps your horse stay the most comfortable and sound.

RIGHT: A farrier shoes a horse.

Walker Farm

Sue Walker lives on a 3.5-acre farm with a small barn and attached 12 x 24 run-in shed that can be opened on both ends. Sue rides her mare, Giverny, a 15-year-old Hanoverian/Thoroughbred cross, in dressage and on trails. She also has two Quarter Horses: Rusty, a 14-year-old gelding, and Angel, a 7-year-old mare. The horses all live out 24/7 and have access to the shed at all times. Sue is a natural barefoot trimmer and has been riding horses for about thirty years. There is no arena on Sue's farm, but she has access to nearby trails and has a two-horse trailer that sees a lot of use. She trailers her horses to group trail rides, clinics, and riding lessons regularly.

One of Sue's favorite things about having her horses at home is the daily interaction she has with them. "They are black and white personalities," she notes. "They keep me grounded and honest with myself. My horse and I have a great time alone riding through the woods."

I asked Sue what is the most important consideration for healthy hooves, and her answer was unequivocal: "Environment. Horses cannot live in mud and manure. They don't want to live in a stall, especially one that stinks of urine and manure. They should be given a shed or stall that they can use if they choose. They need 24/7 turnout if possible. They are designed to survive adverse conditions with minimal interference from humans." She noted that for healthy hooves horses also require "proper diet with fresh water, plenty of exercise, and routine farrier visits." Sue recommends using firm, abrasive materials in paddock footing, such as gravel, sand, or stone dust with 1/4" crushed rock. "Grassy pastures are great," she notes, "but they don't help to keep the hooves hard and comfortable on gravel roads. If you want a horse to be happy barefoot, I believe that they need to live on the surfaces that we want to ride them on. I have five different surfaces in my large paddock area. They seem to do really well on the firmer footing when we are out trail riding." In addition, Sue lives on a dirt road, so she can condition their hooves by riding them regularly on the hard surface.

Sue also described farms that she sees in her daily hoof care practice that she considers to be examples of ideal setups: "A lot of the barns I work in have stalls that access the pasture so the horses can come and go as they please. They have a place for the vet or farrier to work that is safe—that is, large enough, under cover, well lit, flat and free of debris and tools. This is very important since the weather can change and rescheduling can be difficult during certain times of the year." In reviewing your horse's environment, Sue advises considering, "Would I want to live in this stall or pasture? If not, what would make it a more pleasant place for the horse to be?"

Dental Care

It is easy to overlook the importance of the horse's teeth. They are so far up in that big head, we never really see or think about them unless there is a problem. However, horses need regular maintenance of their teeth for good health and comfort, just like they need regular hoof care. Fortunately, most horses only need the attention of an equine dentist once a year rather than every six weeks, as with hooves. (Note that some horses, such as young or old horses or those with dental problems, may need to be floated every six months; your dentist will advise you about your particular horse's needs.)

Horses' teeth erupt continuously throughout their lives, meaning that they are constantly growing and being worn down by regular use. Due to the genetics and relatively soft diet of the domesticated horse, the teeth wear unevenly, resulting in sharp points, hooks, and other irregularities. Left unattended, these irregularities can cause painful sores inside the mouth, discomfort while wearing a bit and bridle, and inability to chew thoroughly. The results you will notice in your horse are a sour attitude, fussiness or resistance to the bit while being ridden, weight loss, and general poor condition.

It's easy to avoid these many problems. Simply schedule an annual appointment with a good, well-recommended equine dentist in your area. The dentist will use specialized tools to "float," or file down, the sharp points and irregularities in the teeth, creating a balanced chewing surface and realigning the teeth and jaws. This kind of regular care is extremely important for your horse's long-term well-being, as poor or inconsistent dental care early in life sets the horse up for more serious chronic dental problems as he ages.

Most veterinarians will float your horse's teeth for you, but this may not be the best choice. Vets may sedate the horse as a matter of routine, while many horses willingly allow dental work without sedation. A veterinarian's training focuses on treating medical problems in the whole horse, so his or her dental training and experience are likely not nearly as thorough and specialized as those of a well qualified dentist. Nevertheless, a vet is likely to charge more for his services than a dentist. Ask around among horse owners in your area to find out whom they recommend for good dentistry.

Like many aspects of horse care, the neglect of dental health is a false economy. An annual floating costs under $100, depending on where you're located, who is doing the work, and whether sedation is needed. (I recently paid just $55 per horse, but I'm in an area of the country where these types of services tend to be less

RIGHT A speculum allows the dentist access to the horse's molars.

costly.) In comparison, *not* performing an annual float may cost much more in the long run. If a horse can't chew his hay thoroughly, he will not be able to keep weight on. The puzzled horse owner doesn't know the true cause of this "mysterious" weight loss, and starts feeding her horse more and more grain, trying to compensate. Meanwhile, the horse develops some bad habits under saddle, tossing his head and resisting the contact, so she schedules a few extra sessions with her horse trainer. You can see that the extra bags of grain and extra training will quickly add up to much more than the cost of a simple annual float that could have prevented all this distress.

Dealing with Death

There comes a time in every horse's life when a decision has to be made. Perhaps the horse is suffering from a severe colic, and the only options are high-risk surgery or euthanasia. Perhaps the horse has sustained a painful injury with a poor prognosis for recovery. Perhaps he's simply very old, very arthritic, and doesn't enjoy life anymore. A peaceful, painless passing in the comfort of his own home, surrounded by loving caregivers and companions, is perhaps the ultimate gift we can give to our equine friend. This is a decision to make in consultation with your vet, but it is also a very personal decision. Only you and your horse know when the time has come. Generally speaking, when pain or illness have made his quality of life very low, and prognosis for recovery to a comfortable condition is remote or nonexistent, it is time to consider euthanasia. Remember that horses have no concept and therefore no expectation of "tomorrow." They live in the present. And if that present is painful, with no hope of cessation of pain, then there is only one right decision.

Contact your vet to discuss your options and schedule the time. Make your horse's last days as pleasant as possible, with lots of grooming, grazing, treats, and love.

It's not a happy topic to discuss, but there is an important technicality when euthanizing a horse—they're really big. You need to have a plan for what to do with the body. If you have a large enough property and local regulations permit it, you can use a backhoe to dig a large grave. (If you don't have one, rent one or hire someone local to do the job for you in advance.) Euthanize the horse as close to the grave site as possible to avoid excessive, well, dragging.

If it's not possible to bury the horse on your own property, a rendering service may be available to come and haul it away. Schedule this pickup when you make your appointment with the vet, so you won't have to deal with this unpleasant detail at the last moment, while you're grieving. In some areas it is also possible to have a horse cremated, although this is probably the most expensive option available, generally ranging from $500 to $1,000. A final choice is to donate the body to a university vet school, which will use it for research. This option can offer a nice sense of closure, since you know your horse's remains will be serving a greater purpose and possibly helping to save or improve the lives of other horses in the future. (A list of universities that offer this option is available here: www.vetsfor equinewelfare.org/veterinary-medical-schools.php.) Your vet will know what services are available in your area and will help you decide which option is right for you.

12. Handling and Riding

"Light off the leg, soft in the hand;
Ride the horse and not the plan."
—Unknown

Handling Your Horse

EVERY TIME YOU ride or handle your horse, you are training him. He is learning either to respect you or not. Horses are extremely large animals with hard hooves and sharp teeth. If they learn to disrespect people, they can become unruly and dangerous. It's a vicious cycle—an owner lets her horse get away with some inappropriate behaviors, the horse starts testing the waters by threatening to bite or kick, the owner becomes frightened and backs off, and suddenly the horse knows he is bigger and stronger than you. This is not because horses are inherently malicious or because they want to bite and kick us. It's because, as herd animals, they need a leader. Most horses actually prefer to be the follower, but if the human doesn't step up and act as a leader, the horse assumes it's his job to become the leader of your little herd of two. This doesn't mean that horses need to be bullied and dominated into submission. Consistent, firm, yet gentle handling is most effective.

For a difficult horse or a novice owner who needs help learning about horse–human communication, clinics and training opportunities exist, especially within the field of natural horsemanship, which emphasizes handling and ground training (see below). However, opportunities for training your horse on the ground occur multiple times a day every day.

Expect and demand obedience when leading, grooming, tacking, tying, or working around your horse. Again, a gentle yet firm hand is best. Insist that your horse walk at your side when being led, rather than lagging behind or surging ahead. Insist that he stand quietly while being groomed. Insist that he pick up his feet promptly when you request it. Correct disobediences immediately to prevent further problems from developing. Most horses will be happy to know that they have such a strong and consistent leader keeping them safe and telling them what to do, so this kind of handling actually helps them relax. A few horses may try to "test" you more often, and may require an even firmer hand. Just as with riding, if you ever find that you're afraid of your horse, seek professional help from a trainer who can work with you and the horse to get you back on the right track. Fear is detrimental to your relationship with your horse, and will only cause his behavior to worsen when he sees that he's in control.

BELOW: Horses establish leadership using body language, such as this bite threat asking the less dominant horse to move away.

Rules of Thumb for Horse Handling

- Never interact with a horse when you feel fear or rage. Take a step back, walk away, and calm down before moving on.
- When disciplining a horse, there must always be a "right answer" for him. There must be a correct way for him to behave that makes the discipline stop.
- Physical discipline is only appropriate when the horse threatens you first. Do not strike your horse for not standing still, for not being attentive enough, for not backing up quickly enough. A bite or a threat to bite may be met with a prompt, firm smack on the nose and a firm, "No!" A kick or threat to kick can be addressed with a verbal correction or growl and a smack of a crop on the offending leg. Don't let these behaviors go. They will only escalate.
- Discipline must occur within three seconds of the infraction for the horse to be able to make the association with his behavior.
- Always end a training session on a good note, whether riding or doing ground work. If you or the horse become frustrated or upset when trying to learn a new skill, go back to something easy and familiar before finishing your training session to boost your confidence again.

Lungeing

Lungeing is a very useful tool for horse training and exercise. It takes a bit of practice to learn to do it well, but once you've got the hang of it, it's not difficult. The basic concept is to work the horse in a large, 20-meter circle on a long line attached to the bridle, halter, or lungeing cavesson (a special type of halter used for lungeing). The person stands in the center of the circle and uses voice, hand gestures, and cues with a lunge whip to communicate with the horse and ask for transitions. Variations include free lungeing, in which a lunge line is not used and the horse is loose in an arena or round pen, and lungeing with specialized equipment such as side reins, which are attached from the bit to a saddle or surcingle and encourage the horse to seek contact with the bit. Lungeing should be done in an enclosed space with good footing, such as a round pen or arena. Slippery or uneven footing is dangerous when lungeing.

Have an experienced person show you how to lunge before you try it yourself. Most well-trained horses already know how to lunge, but if your horse doesn't, have a trainer work with the horse a few times until he gets the idea. Since it involves constantly working on a relatively small circle, lungeing can be hard on a horse's joints. Change direction often, give the horse frequent walk breaks, and keep lungeing sessions to about 20 minutes or so. Young horses with developing bodies (those younger than three) should only be lunged very lightly, if at all.

Reasons to Lunge a Horse

- Teaching verbal commands—walk, trot, canter, easy, whoa—as well as the concepts of wearing a bit, contact, and roundness for a young horse.
- Reinforcing the horse's response to a forward command.
- Establishing or reinforcing the leadership role of the human.
- Exercising a horse when you don't have time to ride or can't ride.

- Taking the "edge" off a hot or fresh horse before mounting.
- Warming up a stiff horse before mounting.

How to Lunge

Tack up your horse: You can lunge a horse in nothing but a halter, or you can use a bridle or a lungeing cavesson. If using side reins, you'll need to have a surcingle or saddle on the horse as well. The side reins are attached to the surcingle or saddle and then clipped to the bit after the horse has warmed up a little without them. Use of this gear can be complicated, so have a professional show you how to use it and how to make sure the side reins are properly adjusted. Many people like to put boots or polo wraps on a horse for lungeing to prevent injuries from interference.

Attach the lunge line. If using a halter, clip it to the lead-line ring or to the metal bracket on the near side (the same side where you will be standing; you'll have to switch it to the other side when you change directions). If using a bridle, either add a halter over the bridle to attach the lunge line, or run the lunge line through the near bit ring, over the horse's poll, and clip it to the bit ring on the far side. Never clip the line directly to the bit on the near side, as it can pull the bit through the horse's mouth.

BELOW: The lunge line correctly attached to the bridle—over the horse's poll. (Note, however, that this horse's side reins are attached far too low on the girth).

Standing in the center of the round pen or arena, ask the horse to whoa or stand, and let out a little of the line. Facing the horse, hold the lunge line in the hand closer to his head, and the whip in the hand closer to his tail. So if he is circling counterclockwise (traveling to the left), hold the line in your left hand and the whip in your right. Be sure never to coil the line around your hand; if the horse pulls, the coil will tighten and trap your hand.

Point the lunge whip at the horse's hip and ask him to walk on. If he is sluggish, you can pop the end of the whip to make a snapping sound. For a very lazy or disrespectful horse, you can tap the whip lightly on the hindquarters. *Never* use a lunge whip to strike the horse violently. The whip serves as a visual and auditory aid to communicate with the horse; it is not used for punishment.

As the horse walks forward, let out more of the line until the circle is about 20 meters in diameter. Begin walking in a small circle, keeping the front of your body facing the horse and in line with his shoulders. At any time, if you have too much slack in the line, point the lunge whip at the horse's shoulder to move him farther out.

Work the horse at a walk for a few minutes before moving up to a trot. Practice a few transitions between walk and trot, as well as between a slower trot and a more forward trot, before asking for a canter. Work in the first direction should not exceed 10 minutes. Then ask the horse to halt, walk to him, switch your lunge line to

BELOW: Lungeing at the trot.

the opposite side if needed, turn the horse, and work in the opposite direction for up to 10 minutes.

Lungeing Aids

Walk from halt: Point the whip at the horse's hip and briskly say, "Walk on."

Walk from trot or canter: Point the whip at the ground near the horse's head and say "Waaaa-alk." Draw out the word to indicate to the horse that you are asking for a downward transition.

Trot from walk: Lift the whip behind the horse's hindquarters and say, "Trot" or "Teeee-ROT!" Again, you can reinforce the driving aid with an audible pop of the whip if needed.

Trot from canter: Point the whip at the ground and say, "Trrrrrrr-ot," drawing out the word slowly to demonstrate the downward transition.

Faster trot within the gait: Lift the whip behind the horse and say, "Trot on!" Little flicks of the whip toward the horse's hind legs can reinforce your point. A clucking sound is another cue for a faster trot.

Canter from walk or trot: Lift the whip high behind the horse and give it a little swish, while saying, "Cannnn-TER!" Some horses also respond to a kissing sound as a canter aid.

Halt from any gait: Point the whip toward the ground near the horse's head and say, "Whoa" or "Ho."

Slowing down within any gait: Point the whip toward the ground and say, "Eeeeeeasy."

Praise: Be sure to use lots of verbal praise to let the horse know when he's doing the right thing.

Natural Horsemanship

Natural horsemanship is a style of horse training that has rapidly gained in popularity over the past two decades. The basic principle is to train horses in a way that corresponds to their natural herd instincts and body-language-based communication. Although most natural horsemanship programs do include ridden work, much of the focus is on ground work and handling. Training techniques typically include leading exercises and lungeing or round-penning (essentially free-lungeing in a round pen). Therefore, this type of training can be beneficial for a novice owner who is less than confident in her horse-handling skills, as well as for a horse that needs a refresher on respect.

The specifics of natural horsemanship vary depending on the system that you choose. In a departure from most traditional styles of training and riding, each natural horsemanship style seems to be focused around one of several famous clinicians—charismatic characters who travel the country promoting their individual systems, while trying to sell tickets, DVDs, and overpriced training equipment along the way. If you can find a good, solid trainer who follows the principles of natural horsemanship while not trying to sell you a $100 signature lead line, you are on the right track. A good natural horsemanship trainer will teach you to use your body language to demonstrate your leadership role to the horse, and will give you training techniques to practice and develop your horse-handling skills. The bonus is that these techniques are often fun, and can serve as little games to play with your horse.

Trail Riding

Many riders who keep their horses at home are trail riders, either as a secondary or primary pursuit. It's relaxing, fun, gets you out into nature, and doesn't require an arena. Most horses really enjoy trail riding as well. They seem to relish tromping through the woods, smelling new smells and seeing new things. As herd animals, the majority of horses prefer to trail ride with a buddy, but with a little work and training you can convince most scaredy-cats that they are

not going to die if they go down the trail alone.

One of the great things about trail riding is that it can be as mellow and easy or as challenging and athletic as you choose. You can saddle up for a short, quiet amble through the pine trees behind your house, or you can trailer to exotic locales, gallop along the beach, or climb up mountains and down ravines.

Trail riding may be simple, but it's not always easy. Many horses, especially those accustomed to ring work and to always being around other horses, may find the prospect terrifying. Some of the challenges you may encounter, along with solutions, are below.

Herd-bound or nervous horse. The first few times you ride your horse on trails, he may react with fear. If he hasn't trail-ridden before, it is a totally new experience for him. As a prey animal alone in the wilderness, it's totally natural for him to be afraid, nervous, or spooky. Even an experienced horse can develop herd-bound or barn-sour behavior, meaning that he's unwilling to leave the comfort and security of his barn and pasture-mates without putting up a fuss.

For a green horse, it can be helpful to hand-walk him along the trails several times before you try riding. Horses seem to gain a sense of security from the human walking beside them rather than riding on their backs. Whether walking or riding, be sure your body language radiates a sense of calmness and confidence—don't allow fear or tension to creep in. The horse can sense your state of mind, and your confidence will help him relax and settle. Some quiet, pleasant hand-walks through the woods will familiarize him with the new territory and let him know that he doesn't need to be afraid. When you finally mount up and go riding, it's best to go along with a confident, safe older horse for companionship. Again, the other horse's body language and calmness will communicate to your greenie that he has nothing to fear. After a few such positive experiences, it will be vastly easier for your horse to venture down the trails without a companion. Try to make trail riding a fun and happy time that your horse looks forward to.

In the case of an experienced horse that has become buddy sour or barn sour, you need to first assess whether the horse is truly afraid to leave his companions, or if he's just putting up a fight out of sheer cussedness or trying to get out of working. If he's honestly afraid, go back to square one and treat him as if he were a green horse, as described above. If he's just being a bully, you need to put him to work. Use your legs and a crop or whip to "put him in a box" with your aids . . . the only possible way to go is forward, toward the trail. If he goes forward willingly, reward him by relaxing all your aids and praising him verbally and with pats. If he tries to spin or stop, apply the forward driving aids again. Trotting in a circle can serve as a disciplinary tactic—fighting with you means he has to work harder. Walking down the trail means he gets to relax and rest. Similarly, riding movements such as shoulder-in and leg yield can help to make a hot or spooky horse focus on you and your aids, rather than scary things in the woods or his buddies back home. Don't let him win the small battles, or you will end up with a large battle.

Once you turn back toward home, never let such a horse gallop or canter. This can result in a dangerous situation where the horse expects that going toward home means he gets to take off. Again, shoulder-in or leg yield can help refocus the horse and prevent him from trying to bolt toward home. When he relaxes, let him go straight as a reward.

Before long, good, consistent training will result in a horse that calmly, safely, and willingly heads down the trail with you. *Note:* If you find yourself in a situation where you're truly afraid and feel you can't

ABOVE: Hand-walking can give a horse confidence in scary situations, such as learning to cross a bridge.

control your horse, stop trying to train him yourself. Your own fear and tension will only make things worse, as the horse will feed off the tension and become more nervous himself, or even take advantage of your fear to bully you into getting his own way. It's time to hire a trainer to work with the horse until he's safe enough for you to ride.

Traffic. When riding on public roads, even rural or dirt roads, traffic is always a concern. Being hit by a vehicle is a very real danger. Ride as far into the shoulder as safely possible, and wear bright colors to alert drivers to your presence. Try carrying a white dressage whip in your left hand, and let it stick out into the road to force cars to give you a wide berth. If there's a section of road you ride on often, ask the town to provide a "Horse Crossing" sign to warn drivers to slow down and look sharp. Legally, a horse and rider have the right-of-way, but some drivers either don't know the law, or are simply inconsiderate or don't understand that horses are unpredictable. Most drivers, in my experience, will slow down and leave plenty of room as they cruise by, but others may speed past you at close range or even spin out their tires at the worst possible moment. It's up to you to keep yourself and

your horse safe by being as visible as possible and making sure your horse knows how to behave near cars.

Don't expect a horse to simply accept cars flying by without batting an eye. Like anything else scary, horses need to be trained and desensitized to traffic. Before venturing out onto the road, make sure your horse knows how to sidepass or leg yield—that is, to move sideways in response to a cue from your leg. You can't steer your horse to the side of the road using your reins—this will result in his haunches swinging out into the road. A cue for a leg yield or sidepass will allow him to sidle over and keep his butt out of traffic. He also must be unquestioningly obedient to all the basic commands, especially whoa, so he will trust your judgment to keep both of you safe.

Hunting season. During hunting season it's probably best to avoid the woods altogether—a horse is similar in shape to a deer, and hunters are notorious for shooting anything that moves. (Not *all* hunters, mind you. Most are responsible, ethical, and courteous. But here in the great state of Maine, every November the news reports are peppered with tales of people being shot accidentally by hunters who were not being careful enough.) If possible, it's best to avoid trails and wooded areas during these times—stick close to home and ride

FIRST: The view through Robin's ears.

MIDDLE: This horse is moving sideways away from the rider's left leg in a sidepass.

LAST A gallop through the snow on a winter afternoon.

in your arena or on public roads. If you do decide to venture into the wilderness during hunting season, you absolutely must wear as much blaze orange as humanly possible. Helmet covers, gloves, jackets and vests, reins, saddle pads, leg wraps for the horse, and even quarter sheets are all available in blaze orange.

Snow and ice. A layer of soft snow is actually great to ride in. Snow covers up roots and rocks, and makes the woods quiet and beautiful. A trot or canter through a snow-covered field is one of the great joys of horse ownership. Snow deeper than a foot or so is still safe to ride in, but it may be quite a workout for your horse to slog through, so keep his condition in mind as you ride. If the snow is very deep, try using a snowmobile, ATV, tractor, or even a pair of snowshoes to pack down a section of trail to make it easier and more pleasant to ride on.

Deep snow that has developed an icy crust due to thawing and re-freezing is not safe or fun to ride in. Similarly, a thin layer of hard, icy snow is slick and dangerous and should be avoided. High-traction hoof boots or studs in your horse's shoes can make it safer if you feel you must ride when conditions are a little icy, but it's really best not to ride when there's ice underfoot. The risk of the horse injuring himself, or even slipping and falling, is too great.

Every Time, Every Ride

There are currently no laws mandating that you must wear a riding helmet while mounted on a horse. But common sense and safety require that you do. Most English disciplines, particularly those that emphasize jumping, traditionally feature a helmet as part of regular riding attire. Dressage was historically an exception to that rule, with many riders schooling with no helmet and FEI riders wearing top hats at shows. However, recent high-profile head injuries, such as those of top dressage rider Courtney King-Dye, have started to change that trend. Now all riders through Fourth Level, as well as *all* riders under age eighteen regardless of level, at USEF-sanctioned dressage shows must wear helmets, and adult riders above Fourth Level have the option of the traditional top hat or protective headgear.

The vast majority of Western riders do not wear helmets. I'm not entirely sure why that is, but I believe it's mainly just tradition and trend. Recently, most governing bodies for horse shows have changed their rules, which formerly required Western attire including a cowboy hat, to allow riders who wish to do so to wear helmets. Hopefully we are starting to see a sea change in attitudes toward helmets among Western riders.

Still, you will often hear the argument that a rider does not need to wear a helmet because she rides in a Western saddle. I suppose that's because she can grab the horn in the event of a buck or a bolt. But no saddle will protect your head if your horse slips and falls under you, or rears and flips over backward. Many riders argue that their horses are so safe and quiet, there's no risk of a fall. But even under the best of circumstances, stuff happens. Any horse is capable of a spook, a misstep, or even a slip and fall, resulting in an unscheduled dismount for the rider. Above all, it is of the utmost importance that children be taught the value of a helmet and be required to wear one when mounted. You might as well set a good example and wear one yourself.

No one can force you to wear a helmet when riding your own horse on your own property, but there's really no compelling reason not to wear one. Maybe you'll feel foolish in front of your helmetless buddies. Maybe you're worried about messing up your hair. Maybe you enjoy the feel of the breeze across your scalp. None of these really holds a candle to the risk of concussion, traumatic brain injury, lifelong mental impairment, or death. Just wear your helmet—every time, every ride.

Safety Considerations

Wear a helmet. To keep yourself safe when out on the trail, the number one rule is to always wear a helmet. Accidents can happen even on the safest horse, and when outside the ring the chances that you might hit your head on a rock or tree are all too high. If the terrain is quite treacherous or you have reason to believe your horse might be spooky or hot, it's not a bad idea to wear a safety vest as well.

Carry a cell phone. Second, always carry a cell phone *attached to your body*, not to the saddle or the horse. If you fall or otherwise become separated from your horse, your phone won't do you much good if it's attached to the saddle and the horse is hightailing it back to the barn. Stash it in a zippered pocket or a holster attached to your arm, leg, or the back of your belt. (Your hip is not a great place for a phone either—if you fall, you're fairly likely to land on your hip, potentially breaking your phone.)

Wear bright colors. Bright, bold colors will make you more visible in the woods, alerting anyone else out there—hikers, mountain bikers, or hunters—to your presence more quickly. The sooner they see you, the sooner they can leash their dogs, halt their bikes, or, in the case of a hunter, fail to shoot at you. In addition, if an accident were to occur, leaving you incapacitated or unconscious, bright clothing will make it easier for searchers to find you. Whenever you ride on the road, take care to make yourself as visible as possible with bright, light colors so drivers will easily see you and slow down. Reflective material is also beneficial in low-light conditions, such as early morning or evening.

Use the buddy system. Any time you ride out alone, make sure someone knows when you're leaving, when you expect to be back, and where you plan to ride. If you don't return at the expected time, they'll know where to go looking for you. Any time I ride alone (whether on the trail or in my field) I text my husband right before mounting. He knows to expect a follow-up text from me in about an hour to let him know I'm back. If he doesn't hear from me, he calls, and, although we've never had to use this plan, he would come looking for me or call emergency services if I don't answer.

Carry a first-aid kit. For short jaunts, this isn't really necessary, but on a long ride in a large wilderness area, it's wise to carry a small first-aid kit capable of treating human and equine injuries. It can fit in a fanny pack or saddle bag and should include VetWrap, gauze, antibiotic ointment, a sharp pocket knife or Swiss army knife, hoof pick, Band-Aids, epi pen, tweezers, hydrogen peroxide, antibiotic wipes, hand sanitizer, Tylenol, bottled water, and snacks such as granola bars or trail mix.

ABOVE: This rider is well outfitted in bright colors that make her highly visible to other trail users.

Any time you ride alone, make sure someone knows where you're going and when you'll be back.

Hohmann Farm

Nancy Hohmann was born wanting to be around horses. After taking riding lessons intermittently as a child and during college, she bought her first horse at age twenty-three and hasn't looked back. "My first horse was the equivalent of the first car," she laughs, "kind of banged up and old. But he was a great first horse because he taught me a lot. I've had one or more horses ever since then, and—well, that was a long time ago." Nancy is now a therapeutic riding instructor and owns a two-acre property, where she has kept her twenty-four-year-old Quarter Horse mare, Mistel, for fifteen years.

During her life as a horse owner, Nancy has both boarded and kept horses at home. Boarding does have its advantages, she admits. "With small kids, it was very convenient. I could put the kids on the school bus in my riding clothes and go riding," she recalls of the three-year period when she boarded her old Morgan gelding at a small facility in Montpelier, Vermont. "I didn't have to worry about whether it was time to feed the horse, get the horse in or out, or buy hay, or whatnot." Nevertheless, Nancy says it is her preference to have her horse at home. "I may not ride her every day, but every day I see her, talk to her, brush her, feed her. Last night was a beautiful night, so I just went out and found her in the field to talk to her. Just hung out. Tonight it's supposed to be nice again, so I might ride her in the moonlight. You can't do that kind of crazy stuff if you're boarding."

"And now with the grandkids," she adds, "it's so nice to have her right here, so if it's raining or something they can just play with her and brush her in the garage." Mistel has free access to her pasture, and the door is always open to her stall, which is in the back of Nancy's garage.

Last year, Nancy had a small riding arena built in her pasture. "Like everything," she sighs, "it cost twice as much as what you figure it's going to cost." She is still happy that she made the choice to put in the arena, because she uses it often. She rides in her arena during hunting season when it's not safe to trail ride, with her young grandchildren, or when it's raining. "It doesn't get heavy use, because my primary joy is trail riding," Nancy notes. "But because the logging truck traffic on this road has increased so much, it's safer to ride in the ring. On days when the trucks are on parade I just ride in the ring. And I can share it with friends and neighbors, so that is a joy."

In addition to riding on local roads and trails and in her arena, Nancy often joins a friend to trailer their two horses to clinics and to trail riding destinations. "We go to Acadia [National Park] and camp and ride the carriage roads. That's the most fun. Last year we went with a friend and we stayed for a week. I've ridden on Popham Beach and Scarborough Beach. With my Morgan, I used to take him in the trailer with a jog cart, with two little kids at the time. I'd plunk them in the cart, hitch him up, and go driving."

An interesting point about Nancy's style of horsekeeping is that her mare, Mistel, lives alone without a companion. Nancy has kept one to two horses at a time at her home, but she feels that Mistel is actually happiest alone. Mistel shared her pasture for five years with a young Morgan, named Tally, that Nancy had bought after her older one passed away. Tally was much more rambunctious and high-strung than Mistel. Nancy recalls that she wasn't able to ride him away from the farm without Mistel because he would get too upset. Eventually Nancy decided Tally was getting to be too much horse for her, and she sold him to a nearby dressage stable. "I swear," Nancy recalls, "When Tally got on that trailer for the last time, Mistel breathed a sigh of relief." Tally and his antics had been stressing her out. Mistel became much more relaxed with her pasture to herself.

Not every horse is happy living alone. But for some horses, like Mistel, it's an acceptable lifestyle. This is an example of why it's important to take each horse's needs into consideration when designing your farm and management strategies—every horse's needs are unique. "Some people think I should get a donkey," jokes Nancy, "But that's the last thing I want to do! Look, if she were pining away, I'd be out there looking for another horse. But she's fine."

I asked Nancy if she'd ever consider going back to a boarding stable. Her answer: "When I get too old to shovel manure, yes. If it gets to the point where I can't ride anymore, I'm done. Because that's one of my greatest pleasures, is riding a horse." What is it about horses that's so important to her? "Oh gosh. Everything. The way they smell. When my daughter comes home, she says she's happy to smell the horse again; she doesn't have one right now. I think having a horse is very therapeutic. Riding a horse, I don't have to be off galloping . . . as soon as I throw my leg over and sit down, I feel better. Brushing a horse is very calming to me. Many mornings I sit and read to my horse, and she enjoys that. I often used to say if I didn't have a horse, I would be in psychiatric care, and that's true. So pricewise it kind of evens out! But having a horse is a lot more fun."

Example Riding Schedule—Eventer

Sunday	Light hack on trails
Monday	Ride on dirt road; work on leg-yields and shoulder-ins
Tuesday	Ride on dirt road; conditioning
Wednesday	Ride in field; work on stretching and relaxing
Thursday	Day off
Friday	Hack on trails; pop over some cross-country-type fences
Saturday	Dressage lesson; ship in to trainer's arena

Making Do

Not every home horsekeeper has an arena—in fact, it's likely that the vast majority do not. An arena, if constructed correctly, is very expensive and takes up a lot of valuable space. Many riders may find that their limited resources are better spent in other ways—the space can be used for more pasture, and the money can be spent on hay, lessons, training, a trailer, a tractor . . . The fact is, an arena is a luxury item above and beyond the basic luxury of keeping our horses at home in the first place. If you don't have an arena on your property already and can't justify the expense to build one, don't despair. There are lots of options. Consider your existing resources. A nice wide trail or a dirt road is perfect for schooling lateral movements for dressage, working on canter sets for cross-country conditioning, or enjoying a pleasant hack. You can add natural jumps with go-arounds in spots where the footing is good. Use a fallen log, a rock wall, or a stack of well-secured tree limbs as a jump. Just be sure you have plenty of level, solid ground for takeoff and landing.

Riding on the road is also not out of the question. As long as the road is relatively safe—with a wide shoulder, a low speed limit, and not too much traffic—there's no reason not to ride on the road. Just make sure your horse is safe, well trained, and desensitized to traffic.

BELOW: Schooling dressage in an open field, a slight incline encourages Robin to really engage her hind end.

Wear brightly colored clothing, or even add reflective strips to your helmet and vest. See page 231 for more safety tips on road riding.

An open field can be useful for most types of "arena" work—jumping, dressage, or Western. Even if it's not perfectly level, the hills can actually be a boon, working the horse's back and hindquarters and helping him learn to balance as he negotiates the uneven terrain. I've found that after riding awkward 20-ish-meter circles over the rolling terrain of my field, a true 20-meter-circle in a nice, level dressage ring at a show is a piece of cake.

You'll need to pay a bit more attention to the weather and conditions if you're riding on grass—if it's wet, it's going to be slippery and perhaps muddy. I don't ride in my field at all if it's wet. I just head down the dirt road on those days. The area you plan to use as a pseudo-arena should be as level as possible, and as close to 20 meters wide as possible to approximate the standard riding arena. The soil should be more sand than clay, which will allow it to drain well and resist muddiness.

If there's truly nowhere decent on your property to ride, consider trailering out to a nearby arena. Most trainers are happy to have you bring in your own horse for riding lessons, and many will also let you school in the arena on your own for a small fee. This way you can get in several "real" rides per month in an arena, and use your remaining riding time at home to work on the trails.

Training Problems

Even a well-trained, older horse can develop some behavior problems under saddle if he is ridden inconsistently or by a novice rider. In many cases, you may be able to nip these issues in the bud, with help from a good instructor who can offer advice as you work through the problem. In more extreme or ingrained cases, the help of a professional trainer is warranted. If you find you are frightened of your horse, discuss with your trainer the possible outcomes. The trainer may feel she can work through the problem with the horse and return him to you as a safe mount. Or, she may feel the horse is not a good match for you on a more basic level—his temperament may simply not mesh with your confidence level and abilities. In that case, there's no shame in considering selling the horse to a more appropriate rider, with full disclosure of his behavior problems and triggers.

One of the most important things to do when faced with a training problem is to rule out pain as a cause. Many painful conditions can cause resistance—if it hurts, the horse is not going to want to do it. Work with your vet to rule out joint problems, hoof problems, diseases such as Lyme disease, chiropractic or muscular problems, ulcers, reproductive system pain in mares, and anything else that the horse's behavior might indicate as a problem.

The Spooky Horse

Some horses are very spooky, and others are not. To a large degree this is simply a matter of innate temperament. However, there's a lot you can do to minimize spooking even in a sensitive horse. One of the first steps is to desensitize the horse to a variety of stimuli. Desensitizing means exposing the horse to a stimulus repeatedly until it becomes "normal" and no longer frightening to the horse. I don't necessarily advocate tying a bunch of junk onto your saddle and chasing the horse in a round pen as a way of desensitizing him. This can often backfire, terrifying the horse instead of calming him. Instead, try to expose him to new sights and sounds as a regular part of his daily life. Don't shield him from such things as tractors and machinery working, cows or deer near the pasture, laundry flapping on the clothesline, and so forth. Try to get him out of the arena and off the farm as early and often as possible. Plan trips to nearby farms for clinics or pleasure rides, go on trail rides off property, and otherwise expose him to as many new places, horses, and people as possible. This is known as putting miles on a horse, and results in an animal that takes everything in stride and is not frightened or upset by new and different experiences.

When your horse does become nervous or spooks at something, your first priority is to stay calm yourself. A horse's natural instinct is to feed off the emotional state of his leader—if you become frightened of your horse's behavior, all he will know is that you're scared, so there must be something dangerous nearby that might eat him. Conversely, if you exude a sense of confidence and calmness, the horse will feel that everything's going to be okay, even if he's scared, because you, the leader, are in control. This will help him calm down more quickly. A few gentle strokes on the neck and soothing words spoken in a calming tone help too.

Note: Excessive spookiness can often have a physiological cause. Vision loss, hearing loss, intermittent pain, chronic muscle tension, and certain nutritional imbalances can all cause a horse to be spooky and nervous. If a previously calm horse suddenly starts spooking, or if the spooking seems excessive and can't be controlled through training, consult with your vet to rule out these problems. Sometimes diet can be directly related to spooking—if a horse is getting too many calories from grain and sugars, or is eating certain types of feed such as alfalfa, he may react with excessive anxiety. Modifying the diet or adding a calming supplement can help in these cases.

Resources

BOOKS

Getting Started

Folse, Melinda. *The Smart Woman's Guide to Midlife Horses*. Trafalgar Square Books, 2011.

Hill, Cherry, and Richard Klimesh. *Equipping Your Horse Farm*. Storey Publishing, 2006.

Hill, Cherry. *Horsekeeping on a Small Acreage, 2nd edition*. Storey Publishing, 2005.

Shiers, Jessie. *101 Horsekeeping Tips*. The Lyons Press, 2005.

Shiers, Jessie. *25 Projects for Horsemen*. The Lyons Press, 2008.

Training and Handling

Bell, Jaki. 101 Schooling Exercises for Horse & Rider. David & Charles, 2005.

Bucklin, Gincy Self. What Your Horse Wants You to Know. Howell Book House, 2003.

Jahiel, Jessica. Horse Behavior Problem Solver. Storey Publishing, 2004.

Marks, Kelly. Teach Your Horse Perfect Manners, Trafalgar Square, 2010.

McNeil, Hollie H. 40 Fundamentals of English Riding. Storey Publishing, 2011.

Parelli, Pat. Natural Horse-Man-Ship. Western Horseman, 2003.

Savoie, Jane. Cross Train Your Horse. Trafalgar Square, 1998.

Horse Care and Health

Equine Research. Horseman's Veterinary Encyclopedia. The Lyons Press, 2005.

Gore, Thomas, DVM. Horse Owners' Veterinary Handbook. Howell Book House, 2008.

Kellon, Eleanor M. Horse Journal Guide to Equine Supplements and Nutraceuticals. The Lyons Press, 2008.

Loving, Nancy S., DVM. All Horse Systems Go. Trafalgar Square, 2006.

Morgan, Jenny. Natural Healing for Horses. Storey Publishing, 2002.

Myers, Micaela. Knack: Leg and Hoof Care for Horses. The Lyons Press, 2008.

Shiers, Jessie. Knack: Grooming Horses. The Lyons Press, 2008.

Thomas, Heather Smith. Horse Conformation Handbook. Storey Publishing, 2005.

MAGAZINES

Dressage Today

Articles on news and training in the dressage world.

Equus

A good resource for keeping up to date on the latest in horse care and health issues. Non-discipline-specific.

Horse Journal

Horse care and health information, featuring unbiased reviews of horse care products and equipment.

Horse & Rider

A focus on Western riding, training, and horse care.

Practical Horseman

Articles on news and training in the English disciplines, including dressage, eventing, and hunter/jumper.

Western Horseman

Training and horse-care information from a Western perspective.

WEBSITES

www.chronofhorse.com: The online version of The Chronicle of the Horse magazine, featuring show results and news about dressage, hunter/jumpers, eventing, and steeplechasing. It hosts an online forum at www.chronicleforums.com, which is a fabulous community of knowledgeable horsefolk.

www.dreamhorse.com: A useful website for searching for sale horses.

www.dressagedaily.com: News and results from the national and international dressage arena.

www.equine.com: Another popular and useful national horse sales site.

www.equisearch.com: The online portal for several horse magazines, including Equus, Practical Horseman, Horse & Rider, Horse Journal, American Cowboy, and Dressage Today.

www.eventingnation.com: A popular blog-style site featuring national eventing news and results.

www.horsecity.com: A site popular among Western and natural horsemanship-oriented riders, which also hosts a vibrant community forum.

www.thehorse.com: The online edition of the well-respected magazine The Horse, featuring the latest research and information on horsekeeping and horse health.

Index